Trump's Christian America

vs

<u>ALL</u>

ARE CREATED EQUAL

Day of Judgment

The challenge to restore 'the soul of a nation' to itself & to restore its civil promise to the world

The Last Spiritual Samurai

An American citizen stands up

Dedicated to my grandchildren & their future

*(Listen my children: Mother's teach us the secret of the cosmos... **the sacred rhythm**, that becomes music... & life.)*

Be advised to let no racism, religious intolerance, political ideology or personal experience to tempt you to scorn God's Way- your parent knows your suffering & suffers more...

Remember, you were 1st of all God's children & must yet return to that status. Do not suffer to learn the art of self-deception. It is an even greater enemy to you than the slave owner who keeps you in psychological & physical bondage.

Instead, learn the sad lesson the child denied & abused must suffer when they, too, rebel, but to reject. For them, too, all seems lost & without morally significant comfort or options. Then, we are most tempted & most certain to kill our brother, as Cain came to kill Abel. For if we allow our past to dictate the path of the present, to choose to call for the blood of those who have oppressed us, we will discover too late, that the blood of a brother, cast upon the sands of time, cannot be erased. But only remembered.

Common Sense

II

"All interpretation of meaning, like all scientific observation, strives for clarity & verifiable accuracy of insight & comprehension. The basis for certainty in understanding can either be rational, which can be further subdivided into logical & mathematical, or it can be of an emotionally empathic & artistically appreciative quality... The highest degree of rational understanding is attained in cases involving the meanings of logically or mathematically related propositions; their meaning may be immediately & unambiguously intelligible." Max Weber

Table of Contents

Getting it straight: Racism & sexism are neither protected behaviors nor protected rhetoric/speech

The Alpha Configuration Patriot & Nation: I defend America's 1st value to the whole world, starting in my family

The 3 Great Human Virtues in the Time of the Global Patriot: For whom the bell tolls

Special offering
A Personal Letter to 'white' Christians, from Jesus

Book 5
Movement towards global righteousness

The Great American Hoax: Socialism as communism & un-American & other children's stories to terrify & divide

Bended knees, raised fists & the true patriot in the times of trouble: Remembering the righteous rebels King, Gandhi & Camus

Even as enemies, arm in arm, we integrate: The social legacies of Sun Myung Moon & Jesus

"Peace Starts with Me" as providential & global movement towards community: the need for the certainty of morally significant values informing our emotional identities

Thoughts at the meridian

The greatest threat to world peace: Trump's 'Christian' America as the failure to defend the true values of America in the moral confrontation with China & Russia

Conclusions

A personal introduction & appeal:

4 Words that saved… & save a nation, each day, to this day

"I was delivering a vehicle for a company to Florida, coming all the way from California, when I noticed 2 ladies in a car on the side of the road. This was before cell phones. I stopped & backed up. I try never to pass a stranded motorist without determining if they need some assistance. As I approached, they both got out of the car. It appeared as they might be mother & daughter. They were also black. As I enquired if I could lend assistance, I noted the concern on the 'mother's' face, but a measured concern, as she took stock of the man in front of her. But I also noted, with some shock, that the younger girl, maybe 17-18, looked at me with abject terror. I have NEVER been reacted to in my life that way. It was a very humiliating experience. As the woman recognized the fear of the girl, where before I had offered to give them a lift or make a call as needed, I saw her relief as she hit upon a proper resolution. She advised me she had a daughter who was a sheriff in the next county & if I could reach her, they would then be fine. I took the number, glad to both be of substantial assistance, but also relieved to offer such assistance in a way the young girl could accept. I quickly sought an exit to the highway & made the call. Reaching her daughter, she was so grateful for the call. The next day I realized the day before had been Martin Luther King, Jr., Day." I most remember that girl's terror as I offered a ride. It still hurts to think of it." Chris Jordan

"The victims of various types of wrongdoing express the ineffable experience of deep bitterness & helplessness. Such an experience of pain is called *han* in the Far East. Han can be defined as the critical wound of the heart generated by unjust psychosomatic repression, as well by social, political, economic, & cultural oppression. It is entrenched in the hearts of the victims of sin & violence, & is expressed through such diverse reactions as sadness, helplessness, resentment, hatred & the will to revenge." Andrew Sung Park

"The attitude & ethos that distinguish the politics of a civil society is civility, i.e., a solicitude for the interest of the whole society, a concern for the common good. The civil person, when he has to decide & act in a situation in which there is conflict, thinks primarily of the civil society as the object of obligations, not of the members of his family, or his village, or his party, or his ethnic group, or his social class, or his occupation." Edward Schils

"Civility in private life & civility in the face-to-face relations of participants in public life are NOT essentially different from each other." Edward Schils

"Whom would take knee in repentance, for harms created, offers no power to others, but to oneself, offers no honoring but to self, where the 1st betrayal occurred, hence, the 1st debt to be paid." Chris Jordan

"These are the times that try men's souls; the summer soldier & the sunshine patriot will in this crisis turn from the service of his country, but he that stands it now deserves the love & thanks of man & woman." Thomas Paine

"We need today... a means to awaken a sense of shame within the oppressor & challenge his false sense of superiority. But the end is reconciliation, the end is redemption, the end is the creation of beloved community... It's love which will bring about the miracles in the heart of men." M.L. King, Jr.

"... (we have) consistently defended justice while exposing fraud, corruption, & other social ills." Hak Ja Han Moon

"To restore the soul of a nation" …quite a declaration as to the social state of a nation, now presumed to have been not only accused, but also convicted & thus, now awaiting an appropriate sentencing.

Fact: America is horribly off course. Morally & therefore by any other socially significant measure. The world now knows it, if there was ever really any doubt.

Fact: Americans betray daily… & have betrayed, with 'pride,' the most important four words to be included in the Bill of Rights & Constitution.

Fact: there is a religious movement in America, seeking to betray & divert the very nature of the country away from 1st principles such as "ALL.. are created equal". They seek to establish a particular form of religious test for citizenship. Establishing such a power base that ONLY a particular interpretation of religion will be allowed to influence all social & legal policies.

Fact: The betrayal of such a value orientation, as is inscribed in such words as "ALL… are created equal", is the line in the sand that separates the patriot from his consumer counterpart, the citizen or other social agents, NOT SO COMMITTED TO THOSE VALUES DEMANDED, rather seeking to force a new standard for defining the true American patriot.

Fact: We are so apathetic & uncaring that we ignore such politically significant social civility, it now beyond any normal, current or morally significant considerations, hence, we just continue on our way.

Fact: I am part of that problem.

Conclusion; my 1st social act MUST then to be to offer repentance, aimed at not only the deepest change of heart informing values, but a repentance to be henceforth sealed in behavior, to counter the unconscious habits of 71 years of living & living indoctrination.

To whom must I repent?

When I was 5, I was sent to a 'black' local church. The black minister taught how Ham's 'sin', at his shame at encountering his father's nakedness, led a God to curse all Ham's ancestors to be the servant of servants… hence, American slavery.

When I returned home, I objected so strongly to this 'morality' that my mother did not dare send me back to that church.

But I soon forgot that experience.

Yet, I have seen the fruit of that history. The black mother, who upon discovering I was the one knocking at her door, when I asked for her son, we having a lunch engagement as friends, inquired as to "Why is this honkie at my front door?" As I discovered, I was the 1st white friend he ever had… he was in college, in San Francisco.

But today… Americans are leading us to a hell such as we have not observed & experienced since Jim Crow was fully flourishing. White Christian Americans are the source & support, economically & politically, for this nationalistic & morally corrupting movement.

Racism, & its siblings. sexism & environmental poor stewardship, are defended & advanced by a people who actually claim a religious exceptionalism & entitlement to such values & use every means, religious, political, economic & plain old stereotypes, to control a system meant to create the 1st truly civilized society.

Thus… before I offer anything else, I offer the deepest repentance, & seek the forgiveness of every African American, every woman/sister, every racial minority or other group that has been victimized by people like me…

Today, I offer a repentance…

A repentance due America… the nation primed to true family values…

A repentance due black Americans; my elders whom have loved & forgiven whites in the silence of aloneness amongst many…

A repentance due black Americans, whose silent suffering is offered up by white Americans as if some measure from God…

A repentance due black America for bearing alone the quality of such forgiveness, the 'acts of love', silently offered for generations…

A repentance due ALL women, my mothers, my sisters, my daughters.

A repentance due all indigenous & other abused minorities, my unrecognized extended family…

A repentance due the earth, as our common birth mother…

Thus, on bended knee, with bowed head, at your feet, I seek forgiveness, your forgiveness…

I offer the ONLY repentance worthy of the word… a repentance birthed in the heart of shame, but a healthy, cleansing shame. This shame acknowledges that 'what I was', what I am, none should have suffered. Hence, today, I need help, I need your help. To become new wine in new wine skin. Today, I need my enemy… to love… & to be loved by.

History now places me before you, & I ask, "Can, will Americans forgive me, by aiding me, to "be all I can be," to you, for you, for myself? This, that I can properly serve you, as you served me, in your silence. Never destroying your enemy, suffering us in a resigned silence. But a silence that once offered, sustains life, even as it is threatened, each & every day.

I cannot offer you anything… for what was taken is not any persons to return, only to acknowledge it should never have been taken… who can return honor not already offered? We cannot… but we can offer it now. By 'being' the dignified quality of human that properly knows its place & thus properly honors all others. In the heart of our behavior. In the quality of civility we offer all others.

Today, I seek to be what I was not before… truly human. Human by how & why I engage all others. America has secured this freedom for me. This blessing that I can now fully engage… to help save America, by living as Americans were intended to live… as an integrated whole.

The promise to you, to participate in such a co-creation as I can muster, as I am, as I struggle to challenge 71 years of bad habits.

But I am but one offering repentance. It was not just me that created this crippled & deviant state, however much I sustained & advanced it. We need a lot of repentance for this nation, its history & the legacy of hate this is still being tendered as an 'American right'.

I discovered something strange… as I repented, as I repent, I sense a quality of self-love seldom offered myself, by myself, much less by this world. I had hope. The past CAN be restored. If restored, the past can be forgiven. The 1st step towards complete community restoration is the desire for healing also. Healing signifies that the relationship has been normalized to its true human potential… that of beloved community. Healing suggests that repentance has been tendered, as a pattern of behavior.

Yet, to repent, to bear true fruit, requires forgiveness. But repentance is also the true measure of the contrite heart, the behavioral commitment to oneself that allows offering to be made in one of the most challenging of moments… when we must own the moral significance of our motives & impact in a shared social environment as beneath both our own needs & the needs of a greater community. A community now impacted by social actions that are hostile to the community environment, as a whole & to its individual parts, thus also impacting its psychology & mores. An environment requiring a more stringent standard of interpersonal moral engagement.

Can white America not only be strong enough to repent those terrible human values such as racism & sexism, can we be humble enough in a true offering of strength & accept the forgiveness that can ONLY BE OFFERED BY OTHERS?

Can white America ask for that forgiveness, an offering of repentance made in rhetoric & social behavior & thus, accept a hand up? Can we DESIRE TO LOVE & BE LOVED BY OUR 'ENEMY'?

Will black America, our sisters & other human family members… would you take my hand, now that I ask? Can you aid my & our mutual recovery to a state of relative psychological health & community? Healing will be individual, community & national in nature, not an even development by any means.

Can black America take the leadership, with women, to offer that which can only be offered? The continued civility that offers we are not only equal, we celebrate that equality in the nature of the values that inform our intercourse & integration? Even with our enemy?

Can we restore the true meaning established, demanded & defended in 4 words… ALL… ARE CREATED EQUAL?

If not… if we cannot find common ground, if we cannot agree to honor the foundations established to create the social environment, where not only is history made, it is restored, then the last few years are ONLY a beginning…

A question of identity or an identity crisis

(or just maybe a question of 'genuine' greatness)

"Perhaps the sentiments contained in the following pages are not yet sufficiently fashionable to procure them general favor; a long habit of not thinking a thing *wrong* gives it the superficial appearance of being *right*, and raises at first a formidable outcry in defense of custom." Thomas Paine

"It is hardly a moral act to encourage others patiently to accept injustice in which he himself does not endure." M.L. King, Jr.

"...(citizenship) implies membership in a community defined by a common substantive end, more comprehensive, more dignified, more authoritative than the particular ends of private individuals." Clifford Orwin

"To love America offers that we have placed all we are, all we have on the table in her defense...then we start with our neighbor as our 1st stop to offer such heart." The Last Spiritual Samurai

"The established religions & their adherents have never realized that man has a central responsibility for turning this evil world around." Rev. S.M. Moon

"... these violent eruptions are unplanned, uncontrollable temper tantrums brought on by long-neglected poverty, humiliation, oppression, & exploitation." M.L. King, Jr.

"There are crimes of passion & crimes of logic. The boundary between them is not clearly defined... We are living in an age of premeditation & the perfect crime. Our criminals are no longer helpless children who could claim love as their excuse. On the contrary, they are adults & they have the perfect alibi: philosophy, which can be used for any purpose—even for transforming murderers into judges." Albert Camus

"This is supposed to be a Christian nation, but tremendous damage has been done to the world... the good Christian moral & cultural tradition is gone... The Protestant & Catholic culture will never do for the future..." Rev. Sun Myung Moon

"The purpose of this essay is once again to face the reality of the present, which is logical crime, & to examine meticulously the arguments by which it is justified; it is an attempt to understand the times in which we live." Albert Camus

(This 3ʳᵈ in a series of white papers, to clarify & defend the original Jesus of human history, not just the Jewish people, offers the social significance of a true Jesus entering into the world through human behavior. America, as the 2ⁿᵈ Israel in a global drama, not to decide the economic future of the world, but the moral & ethical system that will define the human instinct, as a citizen, as a patriot & as a parent, will be explored & extracted. The true moral opportunity provided by 4 words, reasoned by men, that defines the 1ˢᵗ civil right offered EVERY person under its umbrella, citizen or not, that defines all subsequent potential relationships, that offers the world the same experience, is explored for the opportunity & need that remains for its mastery by her citizens. This 3ʳᵈ in the series offers the historical Jesus to the real world. This, as was done by Gandhi & King, offers a new vision for the world... in how we view ourselves, each other & the opportunity between us.

For 6000 years humanity has struggled towards such true integration as to create a sustainable social civility. 2,000 years ago, the nation of Israel had a potential for greatness thrust upon them that was capable of changing the course of all human history. That opportunity slipped between their fingers.

2,000 years later, a nation was conceived that offered the same opportunity for greatness. But that potential greatness is not what is of interest to us. That missed opportunity 2,000 years ago, & the subsequent failure of Christian leadership to inherit the ONLY & PERFECT message Jesus offered, as the concluding thought on the history of moral social development, left open the door for Marxism. That failure was instituted on the basis of the failure of American founders to recognize the absolute obligation to ALL humanity they had, & as much to heaven as to one another.

Slavery was the Achille's heel of America's creation. Its founding failure allowed a birth & rooted such a morally deviant institutional state of mind & unearned entitlement, that even to this day, there has been no national repentance for the slavery that dragged & drags America down psychologically, as well as spiritually, to this day. That failure, of its people, to accept & immediately integrate that 1ˢᵗ Principle of America...allowed a complete failure of comprehension to reach the general populace as to the social significance of that 1ˢᵗ value, one specifically promoting true integration. Hence, today, racists wrongly imagine that their ideas of a morally justified hate are protected by the Constitution, specifically from the wording of the 1ˢᵗ Amendment, in the Bill of Rights.

America, when properly understood... CONDEMNS SUCH VALUES... PERIOD. NO TRUE PATRIOT CAN OFFER SUPPORT

FOR SUCH ANTI-SOCIAL VALUES. We must consent to allow ourselves to understand that the 'normal' values that support slavery, racism, sexism, are the SAME values that link communist, fascist, Nazi & white Christian supremacist into one family of values. Under such an ideological assault, we must consent to integrate a genuinely human standard of rationality to guide our moral compass, given the universal social significance of relationships to human need & meaning. That will be the challenge we engage... & digest.

Today... is now Judgment Day for Trump's white Christian Americans... but not America. She has remained faithful, carrying forward the wisdom of the ages without offering one change of word or intent. But today, in a social & moral climate that challenges all America promised & promises, a new kind of civics discussion is required, as a measure of our assumed, yet to be realized maturity...to restore what has been altered in our understanding, against all indicated wisdom & all evidence.)

You hate Trump & those damn Republicans with their moral heads in the sand? Great! You hate those damn liberal & leftist Democrats & their commie & socialist friends? Great!

Wait a minute here... Can't be right. How can that kind of nation survive long, if that is the civil narrative shared by the citizens, in how they view one another? How to survive this kind of rhetorical social & political reality? Wasn't there some platitude about a house divided?

Then we have people declaring, seemingly without much substance, that America is great & thus, deserves a greater share of the world's wealth & resources... & influence & power. As one administration member noted to the world, "It's America, bitch!"

At this stage, I must confess to just a bit of confusion & thus, humbly needing a bit of defining as to what we will mean when we suggest a nation is 'great' & as such, not only entitled, but maybe even a 'victim' for not being worshipped by others, for our 'greatness'.

We have a POTUS who equivocates legitimate & still much needed morally & providentially significant social protesters with 'sons of bitches.' Yet, this person actually embraces the values that demand the protests! "Racists are 'good' people..." is a mantra now offered as if defending a universal religious value & the perfect embodiment of that value.

As I have participated in a condemning of white Christian Americans with their socially imposed values, then I am challenged as to by what right or authority can I make such moral pronouncement on America & Americans, without exercising the same hubris I suggest we must critique? Simply, I do what ANY MUST, in defense of America.

Questionable? Except in the evidence of the last 4 years…

Four years that argue ALL are NOT equal in America, have never been & should not be so considered.

In contrast, I seek no dominance of others, or for others. This is a defense of each of us…

But the standard of interpersonal consideration I bring to bear, in the moral process of social engagement, as to the meaning & value of the individual, a sacred value denied in history, is now my inheritance I chose for myself. It is also your natural inheritance. Our inheritance. As an inheritance, I am thus naturally entitled & empowered to employ, as you are, the ultimate standard of interpersonal civility.

Where is there such a moral superiority in social opportunity or where is such social civility not only suggested, but demanded as a 1st principle? In 'four' words. But a moral superiority ONLY established in the 'faith' behaviors of its people… as a shared condition of celebration & incorporation. America's unique effort in advancing such values naturally thus defines & defends then not just Americans, but all the people, all the people of the world. Words so framed as to always offer behavioral movement to welcome others, to the same sense of history… that restores the sacred value of the individual, to ALL.

Barring that effort by its citizens? The cost? Look around you…

There is NO IDENTITY CRISIS IN America. There is, however, a question as to the values we have & will continue to engage & employ to honor that 1st civil right & civil opportunity to express patriotism. Our standard of informing values, for the engagement of interpersonal relationships, as the foundation for a morally significant integration into sustainable community, will be measured by the heart of THAT initial commitment... & none other. THAT initial declaration, made by men of contradiction themselves, not only allowed, but rather insisted for a maturing of the species...a moral developing, only needing the right opportunities, values & heart/will.

Yet, today, as we all painfully observe, there is a terrible misunderstanding in America. It is in the nature of a national sin. With global consequences beyond the imagination of the average citizen.

This sin weakens the argument that there is actually a nation seeking such a standard of interpersonal integration & community, a nation of the people, who on the large, offer this as a witness to the world.

INSTEAD, THERE ARE PEOPLE IN THIS NATION WHOM HAVE ERRINGLY, & WITH MUCH ARROGANCE & FALSE PRIDE, TO HAVE ASSUMED A 'RIGHT' TO NOT ONLY BELIEVE IN RACISM... BUT ACTUALLY TO SO INTERPRET THEIR OWN PARTICULAR ENTITLEMENT AS TO INCLUDE THE COMPLETE INTERPERSONAL SOCIAL EXPRESSION & MULTIPLICATION OF SUCH UNIVERSALLY IMMORAL & IMMATURE VALUES.

Defending such values as an 'inheritance' not to be trifled with.

Values ANY rational person MUST acknowledge for the evil it is. For any who 'might' support slavery & racism would never seek to be the one discriminated against. Hence, it is they who defend racism that ultimately offer the greater moral argument as to the evil of racism... & its siblings. For what we would not suffer, for the harm to self or others, inherently argues its moral significance, to one & all.

If we are EVER to demonstrate ANY morally significant intellectual integrity, we much consent to admit that the greatness of America was set back when in the founding of such a nation, such contradictions were ALLOWED to co-exist with those founding words… ALL… ARE CREATED EQUAL"

That moral lapse, all for the sake of an imagined greater profit, an unearned profit, made off the blood, sweat & tears of others, was rationally accessible & recognizable as in conflict with everything they thought to be free of….

Such slavery by others as to diminish the experience of life… denying others a freedom & status NOT to be harmed… by providence or men. Where the founders sought freedom from the ideological terrorism of the state of personal, public & political affairs kings & churches could impose by decree & force, now the founders, in embracing slavery, for its economic value to them personally, failed to honor the God they sought to invoke as the ultimate convening authority for their actions. Hence, where they sought freedom, they would, to secure their own power, come to employ the same values & act in the same way they had been abused… to be the pawns of others, with no moral or legal recourse.

Such hubris then became an entitlement. Justified as if blessed by heaven. For God guided & created this nation… & if we need 'niggers' to make it produce the wealth "WE" want, then God will stand by our sides, this country's existence a matter of God's will… & not merely the will of a few self-entitled men.

Hence, even with the end of slavery, this nation has NEVER REPENTED THE ANTI-SOCIAL & ANTI-HUMAN VALUES & BEHAVIORS THAT CREATED & SUSTAINED SLAVERY.

In this, white churches nation-wide failed in their covenant with God & Jesus. There was no true love conscience in America. Those who were most moved to such justice were in such small numbers & often were cloistered types of communities, seeking to withdraw, not create a new America. There was thus a moral gap in the integrity of our engagement of Jesus.

Hence, no national conscience developed, specifically honoring those 4 words.

If those 4 words are removed?

No end to slavery. No civil rights, no suffrage.

Essentially the state we have right now. Even though laws argue otherwise.

There is still an unowned slavery in America, established in Jim Crow. It is about how certain kinds of employment, once the entitlement of white America in service from 'slaves,' now had to be paid. Hence, 'nigger work' paid now deemed to only require 'nigger wages'. Today, 'nigger work' still exists, still earns 'nigger wages'. People think, act & speak 'nigger' towards others, arguing it is a protected 'right'.

Nope, baby.

Racism, sexism, environmental exploitation, of natural resources or people, ARE THE CURRENT GREAT, MORALLY DEGRADING SINS OF AMERICANS... EMBRACED IN OUR HIGHEST ELECTED OFFICES, IN BANKS, IN CORPORATIONS, IN THE MILITARY, IN OUR POLICE... all those arenas where we have the 'right' to expect the reeling in of such immoral impulses & agendas.

Such a sustained state of mind, of morality & social behavior, **is a form of ideological terrorism... not brought to you by a bunch of socialists & commies; but rather brought to you by white Christians & their secular counterparts.**

Today, the greatest damage done to America, the greatest threat to her internally, the greatest threat to her moral potential to the world... is not from China, the Soviet Union, not by North Korea, though all play their own roles... but the greatest threat to world peace is in the moral failure of the American people... TO BE AMERICANS.

THAT is the challenge before us... to discover, own & live by the principles that define, create & sustain an integrated populace as a nation state/family. Then, & ONLY then may we speak to whether we occupy such a nation, a great nation.

We will be a great nation because of the choices of the values we chose to live by, to define us, by how & why we engage each other & to what effect.

We will be a great nation because we will reveal what any nation, any people, so consecrated & so committed, can create... as a co-statement of not just interdependence or co-existence, but rather... true integration.

This is the heart of humanity in the blood, sweat & tears of history, seeking for their eternal home... on earth. America was the answer to that history. The answer to that hope... sustained & ever defended. The vision of what is possible... for the world.

You want a truly great nation?

Then it is up to us... together.

Only freedom, proper interpersonal true family values, will & heart NOT employed can prevent that us creating that nation..

(Author's note: You will discover I use many short quotes to establish a suggested contributing or defining or concluding state of mind. Other's words often move us beyond the 'me' of every moment we occupy, to an 'us' that cannot be physically observed, but enters the arena of global meaning for humanity. Please, be gentle with me, plow through them, consider them, then observe how they contribute to, help define, clarify & yet, create a sustainable community of ideas that create a new paradigm for integrating into reality with. The human heart (the innate capacity to respond to love offered & to find personal value & meaning in offering love) is as liberated as any rational mind, that rationally engages & recognizes the significance of life around them, & then can morally relate to the wisdom of the cosmos & embrace the inevitable wisdom of heart... I seek to touch & inherit that timeless, global wisdom... Then to whom has been given the authority to deny me? You, as my 2nd self, no less deserving naturally to the wisdom & wealth life has to offer, no less worthy than to any other, must then be offered as I have offered myself... & as I have been offered to. Hence my every effort to rise above the norms of habits of thinking & feeling... but to move towards the heavens in our created meanings that liberate the human heart & mind to its true potential... ONLY REALIZED IN MORALLY SIGNIFICANT SUSTAINABLE INTERPERSONAL RELATIONSHIPS.

Black America, our native Americans, our sisters, all other discriminated peoples have suffered enough for the hubris of a few... Today, Americans speak up... HELP US RECREATE THIS NATION... IN ITS TRUE MORAL POTENTIAL... OR LEAVE.

No room left for slackers... nor time.

Book 1

Behavioral values as foundations for establishing sustainable community

Bell Hooks & a little context: A true righteous rebel offers us her 'heart'

"When I remember all that black & white folks together have sacrificed to challenge & change white supremacy, when I remember the individuals who gave their lives to the cause of racial justice, my heart is deeply saddened that we have not fulfilled their shared dream of ending racism, of creating a new culture... a place for THE BELOVED COMMUNITY." Bell Hooks, feminist, professor, author, human

This single declaration marks the cosmic parameters of Bell's dedication, of heart, of the values that define the essence of the 'who she is', 'how she is', & 'what she is' as she encounters the cosmos & its character actors.

When I first encountered her words, I was profoundly moved. Here was a true kindred soul, so much wiser, more experienced & most important, more caring than I was. She was truly, is truly my elder.

Hence, I owe her a debt. That can ONLY be repaid by sharing a few of her insights, as they intersect this effort, these times, & the challenge of the past, remaining today & shadowing the future already; dimming our hope for substantial change. A needed change in the values that inform our efforts at morally significant integration… not tolerance & accommodation.

In the context of the times, this elder, the direct inheritor of all the hell we, as whites have created, as the 'blessing' we offer to others, as we pass one another by chance, or by design, needs to speak to us, her wisdom.

Her wisdom, the fruit of incredible integrity in the values utilized in her interpretation of & as a result of her digestion of incredible psychological & spiritual pain, may speak to us, or over us, depending upon our commitment & experience to the values that inform her sacred beingness. The result of the choices she made, to continue to care… to love the enemy.

Black American history is the history of forgiveness… a forgiveness given reality in the mothers who had to raise children to face an unholy interpretation of one's value, to oneself & to the cosmos; forced to accept what cannot be accepted, to thrive where there is no nourishment, to create when there is always & only death & the threat of death that is the moment to moment potential one must accept… as one's unearned portion.

But Bell liberates our hope… that WE matter. To each other… 25 years later, her words ring such truth that the mere sound of their utterance rings across that period, to speak just as righteously as the day they were 1st offered to us.

Now, we need her to speak, to us… from the past… yesterday, if one is to measure what changes have occurred since these words were cast to as yet, an ungrateful world.

"The small circles of love we have managed to form in our individual lives represent a concrete realistic reminder that *beloved community* is not a dream, that it already exists for those of us who have done the work of educating ourselves for critical consciousness to ways that enabled a letting go of white supremacist assumptions & values.

"Even though that commitment was 1st made in the mind & heart, it is realized by concrete action, to anti-racist living & being.

"Those of us who are not cynical, who still cherish the vision of *beloved community,* sustain our conviction that we need such bonding not because we cling to utopian fantasies but because we have struggled all our lives to create this community.

"In the segregated South, those black & white folks who struggled together for racial justice (many of whom grounded their actions not in radical politics, but in religious conviction) were bound by a shared belief in the transformative power of love. Understanding that love was the antithesis of the will to dominate & subjugate, we allowed that longing to know love, to love one another, to radicalize us politically. That love was not sentimental. It did not blind us to the reality that racism was deeply systemic & that only by realizing love in concrete political actions that might involve sacrifice, even the surrender of one's life, would white supremacy be fundamentally challenged. We knew the sweetness of *beloved community.*

"I find myself reluctant to 'talk race' because it hurts. It is painful to think long & hard about race & racism in the United States. Confronting the great resurgence of white supremist organizations & seeing the rhetoric & beliefs of these groups surface as a part of accepted discourse in every aspect of daily life in the United States startles, frightens, & is enough to throw one back in silence. NO ONE IN THE DOMINANT CULTURE SEEMS TO CONSIDER THE IMPACT it has on African Americans & people of color... "Africans & Americans who trace their origins to that continent are seen as languishing at a lower evolutionary level than the members of other races." (Andrew Hacker)

"In many ways race talk surfaces as the vernacular discourse of white supremacy. It repeatably tells us that blacks are inferior to whites, more likely to commit crimes, come from broken homes, are all on welfare, & if we are not, still whining & beggin ole massa & kindly miss ann for a hand out.

"Overt racist discrimination is not as fashionable as it once was & that is why everyone can pretend racism does not exist... For some of us talking race means moving past the pain to speak, not getting caught, trapped, silenced by the sadness & sorrow.

"The time to remember is now. The time to speak a counter hegemonic race talk that is filled with the passion of remembrance & resistance is now. All our words are needed. To move past the pain, to feel the power of change, transformation, revolution, we have to speak now-acknowledge our pain now, claim each other & our voices now... sharing a vision of a beloved community where we can affirm race difference without pain, where racism is no more...

"I grew up in the apartheid South. We learned when we were very little that black people could die from feeling rage & expressing it to the wrong folks. We learned to choke down our rage.

"To perpetuate & maintain white supremacy, white folks have colonized black Americans, & part of that colonizing process has been teaching us to repress our rage, to never make them the targets of any anger we feel about racism. Most black people internalize this message well. And though many of us were taught that the repression of our rage was necessary to stay alive in the days before racial integration, we now know one can be exiled forever from the promise of economic well-being if that rage is not permanently silenced.

"Now, black people are routinely assaulted & harassed by white people in white supremacist culture. The violence is condoned by the state. It is necessary, for the maintenance of racial difference. Indeed, if black people have not learned our place as 2nd class citizens through the educational institutions, we learn it by the daily assaults perpetuated by white offenders on our bodies & beings that we feel but rarely publicly protest or name.

"A black person unashamed of her rage, using it as a catalyst to develop critical consciousness, to come to full decolonized self-actualization, had no real place in the existing social structure. I felt like an exile. Friends & professors wondered what had come over me. They shared their fear that this new militancy might consume me... I seemed alone in understanding that I was undergoing a process of radical politicization & self-recovery.

"The intimacy I share with white people now seldom intervenes in the racism & is the cultural setting that provokes rage. Close to white folks, I am forced to witness firsthand their willful ignorance about the impact of race & racism. The harsh absolutism of their denial. Their refusal to acknowledge accountability for racist conditions of the past & present... Racial hatred is real. & it is humanizing to resist it with militant rage.

"Forgetfulness & denial enable masses of privileged black people to live the 'good life' without ever coming to terms with black rage.

"(Black victimization) ... comforts many whites precisely because it is the antithesis of activism. Internalization of victimization renders black folks powerless, unable to assert agency on our behalf...

"As long as black rage continues to be represented as always & only evil & destructive, we lack a vision of militancy that is necessary for transformative revolutionary action... All our silences in the face of racist assault are acts of complicity...

"Rage can be consuming. It must be tempered by an engagement with a full range of emotional responses to black struggle for self-determination.

"Progressive black activists must show how we take that rage & move it beyond fruitless scapegoating of any group, linking it instead to a passion for freedom & justice that illuminates, heals, & makes redemptive struggle possible.

"Many African Americans feel uncomfortable rage when we encounter white supremacist aggression. That rage is not pathological. It is an appropriate response to injustice. However, if not processed constructively, it can lead to pathological behavior-but so can any rage, irrespective of the cause that serves as a catalyst… Until this culture can acknowledge the pathology of white supremacy, we will never create a cultural context wherein the madness of white racist hatred of blacks or the uncontrollable rage that surfaces as a response to that madness can be investigated, critically studied & understood. Denying that rage is at times a useful & constructive response to exploitation, oppression, & continued injustice, but it creates a cultural climate where the psychological impact of racism can be ignored, & where race & racism become topics that are depoliticized.

"Rage about racism in this society intensifies among blacks & our allies in struggle as white denial reaches epidemic pathological proportions. The danger of that denial cannot be understood, nor the rage it evokes, as long as the public refuses to acknowledge that this is a white supremacist culture & that white supremacy is rooted in pathological responses to difference.

"It is useful for white supremacist capitalist patriarchy to make all black rage appear pathological rather than identify the structure wherein that rage surfaces.

"The rage of the oppressed is never the same as the rage of the privileged. One group can change their lot only by changing the system… We need to talk seriously about ending racism if we want to see an end to rage. White supremacy is frightening. It promotes mental illness & various dysfunctional behaviors on the part of whites & non-whites. It is the real & present danger… not black rage.

"Coming to womanhood in the segregated South... facing hardship, the ravages of economic lack & deprivation, the cruel injustice of racial apartheid, I lived in a world where women gained strength by sharing knowledge & resources, not by bonding on the basis of being victims... It was a given that life was hard, that there was suffering. It was by facing that suffering with grace & dignity that one experienced transformation.

"Practically all African Americans experience some degree of racist harassment in this society, however relative, ON A DAILY BASIS.

"Challenging & changing the devaluation of the black womanhood to this society is central to any effort to end racism... Black feminist Ida B Wells suggested that within the sphere of the white supremacist assault on black sisterhood nothing was as hurtful quite as "deeply & keenly as the taunt of immorality: the jest & sneer with which our women are spoken of, & with the utter incapacity or refusal to believe there are among us mothers, wives, & maidens who have attained a true, noble & refining womanhood."

"Collective failure to address adequately the psychic wounds inflicted by racist aggression is the breeding ground for a psychology of victim-hood wherein learned helplessness, uncontrollable rage, &/or feelings of overwhelming powerlessness & despair abound in the psyche of black folks yet are not attended to in ways that empower & promote wholistic states of well-being. Until African Americans, & everyone else in the United States, are able to acknowledge the psychic trauma inflicted upon black folks by racist aggression & assault, there will be no collective understanding of the reality that these wrongs cannot be redressed simply by programs for economic reparation, equal opportunity to the workforce, or attempts to create social equality between the races. Like all mental health disorders, the wounded African-American ps as long as African

Americans rely on existing structures within education & mental health care to address these concerns,"

"By not addressing our psychological yche must be attended to within the framework of programs for mental health care that link psychological recovery with progressive political awareness of the way in which institutionalized systems of domination assault, damage, & maim. Such programs will never emerge wounds, by covering them, we create the breeding ground for pervasive learned helplessness & powerlessness. This lack of agency nurtures a compulsive addictive behavior & promotes addiction. Rarely do discussions of drug, alcohol, & food addiction in black life link these problems to any desire to escape from psychological pain that is the direct consequence of racist assault &/or our inability to cope effectively with that assault. Yet if this reality is not considered then the root causes of genocidal addiction may remain unaddressed.

"Similarly, young black children would not be emotionally crippled by psychological problems that emerge from the low self-esteem, caused by the internalization of racist thinking, if African Americans had institutionalized progressive mental health care agendas that would address these issues so that they would not be passed from generation to generation. The reenactment of unresolved trauma happens again & again if it is not addressed. Psychological woundedness prevents African Americans from engaging in movements for liberation & self-determination that would enhance the quality of our lives as well as our interactions with non-black people. Only as African-Americans break with the culture of shame that has demanded we be silent about our pain will we be able to engage wholistic strategies for healing that will break this cycle.

"WE CANNOT WAIT FOR AN END TO RACIST DOMINATION TO CREATE CONDITIONS UNDER WHICH WE LIVE LIVES OF SUSTAINED WELL-BEING.

"Committing ourselves to living simply does not mean the absence of material privilege or luxury, it means that we are not hedonistically addicted to of consumerism, & hoarding of wealth, that requires exploitation of others.

"The moment any black person embraces black self-determination, a repudiation of victim identity takes place. For at the heart of black self-determination is the political awareness that we must assume responsibility for constructively changing our lives.

Finishing thought...

"When I remember all that black & white folks together have sacrificed to challenge & change white supremacy, when I remember the individuals who gave their lives to the cause of racial justice, my heart is deeply saddened that we have not fulfilled their shared dream of ending racism, creating a new culture, a place of *beloved community*."

Hence, a quarter century ago, one person spoke to a truth & reality that has so little advanced, that EVERY word she utters is as if spoken for the 1st time, to her 1st new audience.

The opportunity to honor all those who passed before, who paid such high prices, while high prices in loss of life & loss of humanity is still escalating, it is also the time...

ML King posed the question: "Where do we go from here?"

It is NOW the Time to Declare....

"To live in anti-racist society, we must collectively renew our commitment to a democratic vision of racial justice & equality. Pursuing that vision, we create a culture where *beloved community* flourishes & is sustained..."

Do I hear an "Amen…"

Inconvenient Truths: A question of individual & species maturity

(Embracing reality & its implied wisdom or the eternal search for knowledge & truth)

"In that the children of Cain have triumphed, increasingly throughout the centuries, the God of the Old Testament can be said to have been incredibly successful." M.L. King, Jr.

"Wherefore, security being the true design & end of government, it unanswerably follows that whatever *form* thereof appears most likely to ensure it to us, with the least expense & greatest benefit, is preferable to all others." Thomas Paine

"Here then is the origin & rise of government; namely a mode rendered necessary by the inability of moral virtue to govern the world..." Thomas Paine

"Fifth Thesis: The greatest problem for the human species, whose solution nature compels it to seek, is to achieve a universal *civil society* administered in accord with the right." Immanuel Kant

The MOST inconvenient truth is generally the one that suggests change we are emotionally predisposed NOT to give any serious attention to. Where that impetus emerges, its source authority, its emotional significance to us, all play a role in our considerations, of any quality. The force of conscience it calls into play is important, neither a plus not minus initially, but rather, when all the relevant 'facts' are in.

We must note with some little surprise that the 1st government is also what we understand as parents. The 1st source for socializing the next generation to the meaning of community, however limited or liberated. Social authority is 1st established as a moral force of consequence, 'judging' the actions & their articulated or merely forced morally significant informing values revealed in the behavior of those being 'socialized'. Hence, all the norms we associate with ANY society finds its ultimate origins in the values informing the social matrix of that founding social system, the family.

Jesus offered that all the law & all the prophets were contained in 2 commandments, that Jesus then held up to his contemporaries as the totality of the evidence needed to understand God's original & sustained will throughout ALL human history. The ONLY addendum he added to that ultimate will was that when encountering the deviant & deviance, our posture would evolve to the same quality of commitment that God had offered humanity since its own departure from principles of life & living; that we love our enemy, seeking their restoration to community, by continuing our own significant commitment to relationship, as its interim protector & steward.

A child learns by listening. If the child is a quick learner, then the child will become an adept listener. This kind of listening is not centered on the ears. It is centered on an unconscious desire/need for community… & all the resources such an aggregate of such an environment, with its relative ecologies, can provide.

We even have 'learned' to listen well enough to pick up on the rudimentary wisdom of the cosmos… in its most basic & primitive forms.

Yet, like a child with little purpose other than self-indulgence, we wander the earth, naming the animals, but learning nothing from them. We see them… but we do not see them in the cycle of meaning they create in their existence & efforts to sustain that existence.

The man fearful observes dominance… interprets that it works. Like the Jewish people who assume if 10 laws were good, then the principle only need be multiplied, to multiply its benefit. But, humanity, like the Jews, discovered trying to control all the variables needed to create a true civility or community may not be merely a matter of willing it so, by law or force. But, they found no relief from want & need so as to reflect on the truly best way forward for humanity, as individuals & as a collective. Force, unwanted, evil, always self-centered & self-serving, force worked. Hence, humanity established a life & life-style not only focused on force & dominance, humanity is convinced there is no other rational option available.

But humanity acted & acts without wisdom.

A wisdom evident in the human body, perfectly worked out in the human eye. A wisdom billions of years in the development… but the human body, the human brain, its pinnacle offering to the opportunity for life to emerge, develop, diversify & specialize.

So, if one were listening, with all one's heart (to care) & all one's intellectual integrity & curiosity, what wisdom might the cosmos offer us?

The 1ˢᵗ Wisdom: The cosmic significance of interpersonal relationships

The 1st Wisdom of Relationships: Integration is the key to sustainable life

The 2nd Wisdom of Relationships: Relationships are about transformation of existing resources & 'social agents' into a particular quality of community, marked by its degree of integration, & hence, rationally accessible moral conceptualizations are revealed in the nature of the integration & its resultant 'creation'.

The 3rd Wisdom of Relationships: Relationships… THIS IS PURPOSE OF LIFE

The 4th Wisdom of Relationships: Conflict, like a wound to the body, is communication to be taken seriously

The Final Wisdom of Relationships: Maturity as the natural behavioral measurement of human social value & status, realized in morally significant sustainable community. The human creation of a 'social form of sustainable life.' In this, then humanity, in the use of reason & the will to care, replicates the very nature & form of the cosmos in its creation of life.

We may talk a good talk, we may use economics & good feelings to distract us, but in the end, we need one another; we are only truly liberated to our full potential in an environment that supports each & every individual as if the last hope for humanity, therefore a treasure beyond imagination.

One may rightly question what kind of leadership we have, what kind of vision & moral paradigm informs their daily activities, especially as it relates to their responsibility to serve their people…

People forget, or do not understand, or are purely into it for themselves, that all leadership, in the end analysis, is little more than acting as a responsible parent would & should act.

We ignore life… we ignore what defines life… we ignore our impact on one another. We shun wisdom, we refuse to engage reality, we write narratives children would not believe.

Jesus offered but one morality, one means to define the child of God… if one does not honor Jesus, in our behavior, like any child does to honor their parent, then one cannot claim to be a Christian much less offer the arrogance that one's nation is superior to others, for this religious designation…

WHY WOULD THE MUSLIM WORLD RESPECT OR HONOR A NATION THAT CALLS ITSELF CHRISTIAN, BUT IN EVERY ENGAGEMENT OF NON-WHITE OR NON-CHRISTIAN, THE BEHAVIOR IS HATE?

WHY WOULD ATHEIST, AGNOSTIC, OR RELIGIOUS COMMUNITY HAVE ANY RESPECT FOR THE PEOPLE OF SUCH A NATION?

WHERE IS THE WITNESS THAT WE PLACE ON OUR RELATIONSHIP TO GOD, IF WHITE HATES BLACK & OTHER RACIAL MINORITIES, WOMEN & ANY IDEOLOGICAL FRAMEWORK EXCEPT THE ONE ADVANCED BY WHITE 'CHRISTIANS'?

Where is the maturity of heart that defines EVERYTHING Jesus advanced?

Repentance, a repentance born in an effort at restoration, is the only hope going forward, the ONLY way to justify a nation daring to call itself… Christian.

Not interested?

Then you are a traitor…

A new covenant: Listening as the 1st & last wisdom in a 'new' rhetoric

(Words only matter because of their shared social meanings)

"Primary among the resources available to the human quest are, of course, those features of its own nature that best equip it respond to the obstacles met in living. The advancement of these characteristics constitutes the evolutionary development of *homo sapiens*. If we can identify these features, we will have located the evolutionary ground of moral value; for such attributes are valuable precisely because they are essential to the continuance & extension of humanity. An individual cannot aim his/her conduct at the survival of the species, but one CAN aim at nurturing those natural capacities upon which species survival depends."
Christopher Lyle Johnstone

"The rebel... demands a certain degree of freedom for himself; but in no case, if he is consistent, does he demand the right to destroy the existence & the freedom of others. He humiliates no one. The freedom he claims, he claims for all; the freedom he refuses, he forbids everyone to enjoy. He is not only the slave against master, but also man against the world of slave & master. Therefore, thanks to rebellion, there is something more in history than the relation between mastery & servitude." Albert Camus

"The most formidable weapon against errors of every kind is reason..." Thomas Paine

The beginning of all Hebrew history actually is founded upon a most important skill set. The beginning of all human history, that engaged & integrated God, involved this same skill set. Every infant employs this same skill set, with all the expertise available to it, at that stage of interpersonal development.

What human social skill is so compelling across so many landscapes?

The capacity for & effort invested in the behavior understood as 'listening'.

This is NOT the casual listening that most of us engage, even in serious situations where nuance, context & motive define the limits of possible social integration, or community.

The infant listens because it is a new experience that is compelling to its whole being. In the listening comes a degree of corresponding rational/intuitive understanding, that is realized on an unconscious level, but to which in time emotional significance is also attached. There are elements of the environment that warrant particular consideration, for the impact they have upon our world. For we have limited mobility. In every sense of the word. We cannot control our body, though we as yet do not comprehend that in such terms. But, we can express ourselves through that limiting medium. Such expression brings response. We note also the pattern of behavior that is productive, our memory fully working, even if not rationally accessible.

The sources of varying experiences respond to the infant. Hence, they are listening. The infant notes the patterns of behavior, both of self & its impact on the environment, hence, the infant is 'listening' too. Cry when one is hungry or tired or needing just to be held, as a surrogate original home, they all reveal an expectation that the 'other' will 'hear', & in hearing, will respond accordingly.

Thus, as the baby replicates communication patterns that are effective to its needs & 'wants', the infant is now participating in the process of community building. The value of a give & take of expression, with morally significant meaning, is established & is established as a social norm. This establishes a social order that the infant is 'socialized' to experience both as a norm, but also establishing such social expectations that the baby will receive such affirmation & cultural & personal nourishment as to allow a 'habit' of behavior, & in time, corresponding motives to develop. Hence, civilization is co-created, the child learning both the significance of community, but also the value & placement of the individual in that ecology (moral configurations of integration in stable social relationships), with its environmental resources (natural or created, physical or cultural).

Childhood is as much about learning the ins & outs of integration, as a full engagement of opportunity or merely the casual form of sustained community, as it is any other socially significant activities. Hence, the 'rules of the game' is very much a major part of the parenting effort. In this, listening is measured in cooperation, creativity of response & sustained compliance. Why the relationship of compliance with listening?

The child MUST learn the need for community, to understand the natural & imposed limits to ideas about freedom that may emerge as we integrate more & more with a greater diversity of others.

Cooperation is the behavioral affirmation that the message of the value & mores needed for integration have been understood & are in the process of also being integrated into our conscience, to further guide our maturing capacity to care for others beyond self-interest. Hence, behavior is the evidence of community, of shared meanings & mores for integration & community. We have 'heard' each other & thus, responded in such form as to establish that mutuality of communication. 'WE' exist, versus a compilation of associated 'individuals.'

In all cases, the caring effort of 'listening', while ultimately in the service of the individual & individual interest, it is also the means by which genuine community is established as a sustained social & politically significant entities, to themselves, & the greater social environment they occupy.

Listening thus can be done as a result of just mimicking others, as in acting like our parents or another person of some significance to us. Listening is also how we learn the ways & means of integration into the variety of community opportunities life will present us. Listening, in its most perfect form, is the conscious & unconscious investment of ourselves into a moment with others. This investment is the fullest measure of the care & quality of care we propose to be the socially significant norm we offer others.

The quality of that investment, is also the social significance we place before others, as our initial offering… & the value we place upon ourselves as an offering to them. People wrongly assume that offerings are ALWAYS indicative of the value we place on the other… but it also signifies the value we equate ourselves to be, in relationship to them.

If I am an honorable person, I offer honorable gifts of attendance. If I am a loving person, my attendance will reflect this experience & value orientation. If I am a hateful person, I may offer hate. If I am manipulative, then my offering will move us in that direction.

In all cases, what we offer one another is meant to be 'heard' & as such, to illicit a corresponding contextually significant social response.

Hearing is the 1st skill we develop, to learn to integrate, to gain community, to whatever benefit we imagine that to be. It is also the 1st act of learning to love… & to be loved.

The commitment to caring in our listening evolves & becomes the mature response of the person who seeks to love, to honor all are created equal, to create community. It is one of the most important of contributing means to conflict resolution & management. It is one of those skills that serve as part of our tool shed for relational maintenance. It is the measure of the quality of attendance we offer other's initially & throughout the course of relationships.

Abraham was in part chosen by 'God' for the ability to listen, as a honorable form of attendance. Moses 'listened' to God & acted according to what he imagined he had 'heard'. A 'master' to be feared & obeyed. Moses listened to God & heard a judge & what MUST BE DONE. Jesus listened to God & heard a 'parent' seeking family.

All three men sought that we would, in turn, listen to them, to inherit what their listening had revealed & thus, suggested was now their course forward. Each asking us to 'hear' them in such form, as to be motived to a further unity of personal & social action.

Later, we are told 3 'wise' men traveled to discover some 'foretold' birth of significance. They were 'listening'.

Prophets emerged in history. People listening…

People caring…

ML King heard a people, who had birthed him & nursed him. He listened…to an Indian, & acted.

People did not want to hear him. People did not want to listen. Enough heard him, though.

Gandhi heard a people, a people who had birthed him & nursed him. He listened to a good Jewish & wise son… & acted.

Some did not want to listen to him. Eventually though, they heard him.

Yet, in every case, the 1st skill is to listen… to learn. To be human means we DO care… or why bother at all?

That's why we MUST listen… even when it profits us not. For in genuine listening, we 1st make the offering of suggesting, behaviorally, that we 'care'.

I listen to you.

I care about you.

Freedom has been engaged.

The depth & breadth of that commitment to care, that commitment to listen, to hear, to integrate… the measure of my humanity. My capacity for morally significant sustainable intimacy & vulnerability the pathways to listening.

Once we have established an absolute standard of care…
to listen, we have established the moral foundation for all
rhetorical exchanges.

Once I have committed to listening, to caring, there is
only one way forward… integration.

THAT TAKES A REAL HUMAN, BEING HUMAN.

Love: the 1st rational act of being human & the mechanistic wisdom of the cosmos in creating life

('We' are, because 'we' chose to be...'this' way, together)

"Sociology... is a science which attempts the interpretive understanding of social action in order thereby to arrive at a causal explanation of its course & effects. In 'action' is included all human behavior when & in so far as the acting individual attaches a subjective meaning to it. Action in this sense may be either overt or purely internal or subjective; it may consist of positive intervention in a situation. Action is social in so far as, by virtue of the subjective meaning attached to it by the acting individual (or individuals), it takes account of the behavior & is thereby in its course." Max Weber

"All interpretation of meaning, like all scientific observation, strives for clarity & verifiable accuracy of insight & comprehension. The basis for certainty in understanding can either be rational, which can be further subdivided into logical & mathematical, or it can be of an emotionally empathic & artistically appreciative quality... The highest degree of rational understanding is attained in cases involving the meanings of logically or mathematically related propositions; their meaning may be immediately & unambiguously intelligible." Max Weber

"In the human being, cultivation of survival attributes has become a conscious end. We can find human endeavor conduct that aims not merely at securing & maintaining personal well-being & continuance, but also at enhancing our natural potencies. We are unique among life-forms on this planet in being able to affect deliberately our own continued evolution... not our physical but... our cultural evolution."
Christopher Lyle Johnstone

"Leadership should not be a question of charisma, how the 'image' affects us as an emotionally significant component, but rather leadership should be contextually considered as a matter of principles to define motive, to inform & guide behavior. This demanded standard of behavior then a sustained state of being expressed across all social mediums of human intercourse, personal social, public & political. Leadership is ultimately about the principles of civility, of parenting & social cohesion. Ultimately, leadership is about establishing community, as a morally significant integration of sacred individuals, into beloved community." The Last Spiritual Samurai

Oh, I can just hear the grinding of teeth & simmering resentment to such a declaration that to love is the 1st rational act of being human. But it is a reasonable observation when all the relevant information is available & considered.

Of course, I have weighted the issue to serve my thesis… that to be human is to care, beyond mere convenience & personal motivations, however clear or muddled & muddied.

But even so, the rationale is reasonable, rational & serves the natural interest of humanity as it intersects species interest.

The #1 interest of humanity?

The values that not only will define the internal nature of every family, however socially positioned, but that will fully define the human, in the context of human need, opportunity & personal & public potential.

The personal, public & political struggles & suffering of humanity, each & every day, the war, pestilence, starvation & other deprivations beyond imagination, are all the compelling & damning evidence we need as to our current standard of individual & universal values.

Those without vision have imagined that for humanity, survival was a matter of domination & subjugation. Humanity looked outside to imagine what it meant & should mean 'to be human.'

But upon reflection, that is a backward way of approaching the question… IS THERE, & IF SO, WHAT IS A HUMAN NATURE?

Yet, the 1ˢᵗ thought then must be to examine not what goes on around us, but rather what are our needs, as individuals & as groupings of individuals.

Obviously, but not obviously, our 1ˢᵗ need is each other, when considered from such a reference point.

The family is an example of a life system like the human body. Everything that takes place within the human body as a living system has a correlative existence in the perfection of the 'body' of a human family. The PRIME factor being the personal & public significance of interpersonal relationships.

There is a mind, that is the central processing system for the body; within our mind, given external stimuli & with bodily needs imposing their votes for attention, various considerations are constantly in flux. Simple ones like the need for sleep, or nourishment or safety from the elements or predators or dangerous physical environments. Then, humans are driven by 'meaning'. Meaning being then rational & emotionally significant assignments of value we place upon events, experiences & people & things.

Parents are the mind of the body of the family.

They gather, regulate the distribution of resources, nurturing & naturing the new 'cells' & orienting them to the 'family environment' with its 'ecology' & various kinds & qualities of resources, natural or created. The new 'cells' are integrated into the system as they are capable of acting in concert with the purposes of the family, as a social system, in a greater environment.

In every movement, in every decision, cognitively engaged, or intuitively or naturally, all life effort centers around relationships… morally significant sustainable relationships.

Not all relationships are equal, not all are directly interrelated. The need to find a new home might not be shared with children, yet the need to include the children as a function of caring for them may be part of the reason for a search for a new home.

Just as significant to the issue of family in the prioritizing of interpersonal relationships, our bodies speak to the wisdom of the universal significance of sustainable & malleable relationships.

Since no two objects can occupy the same space at the same time, every object that exist is always at least slightly impacted different than any other object, even in proximity. That stimulation can induce internal changes or potentials to develop over time. Like rubbing a spot long enough & a number of environmental & individual changes can be induced to emerge. Heat is generated, fire could result, or a destruction of the material being heated by the friction of surfacing integrating, not capable of any other form of integration.

Why are no two snowflakes alike?

Different time, different environment, different stimuli, different ultimate material to work with. Not the same source of 'water'. Thus, the stimulation for development of potential, for the form of the snowflake, will vary just enough in all environmental factors, as to prevent two snowflakes developing exactly the same way, with the exact same resources.

They couldn't.

They occupied a different time environment, the resources to develop cannot be shared or one or the other is diminished in its volume.

Yet, even in the development of uniqueness, the two snowflakes develop because of the same factors, utilizing the same quality of resources to develop, but because of a difference in source material & the time & environment it occurs is not exactly the same, similarities will exist, but not perfect replication of the exact same pattern.

But it is the relationships with the environment that forms that offers a corresponding & parallel nurturing & naturing environment, but one unique to each development. Hence, they all appear as snowflakes, but each unique to its developmental opportunities provided by its environment & own potential for unique expression.

But the critical element is the individual & social significance of integration & 'community', or bonding. The 'morality' is the fact that such development is ONLY realized as a result of interpersonal relationships being engages & sustained as long as the environment can support it & the relationship sustain its own form.

We observe that on every level of the existence of life; interpersonal relationships are the foundation both for existence, but also for development, diversity & sustainability.

The morality of the cosmos in the production of life is a complete witness to the efficacy & value of relationships. Without such principles guiding all such relationships, arms could not become arms, much less could the human body keep communicating those specifications to the next cells that 'evolve' & develop further.

Cells developed along lines that allowed the human body to develop past merely being a mass of cells. Like the snowflake that started as a potential, that given its environment, its own potentials, co-created an ecology where the snowflake co-existed in its environment with all the elements that contributed to its own development plus what else also co-exists in that environment.

In every development of a snowflake, is the evidence of the environmental resources, innate potentials for independent development, & time, that was necessary for the creation an environment where life itself could eventually develop.

That it took over 13 billion years for all the factors to coalesce into an opportunity for life to emerge should not surprise or discourage anyone.

There was no rush.

There was no time clock.

There was no mission.

Just opportunity, resources, potential… & time.

Yet, we have the human eye.

The human body is the 1st witness we each encounter as to the wisdom of relationships, as a opportunity for engagement & integration.

If we understand that there is no human body, no human eye, no fetus, no child, without first the most incredible sequence of events, of interpersonal relationships developing, then we look around, we might make a correlative discovery worth noting, worth considering, for the wisdom it offers.

From birth to death, as a physiological fact or as a matter of human meaning interpreted from events, relationships are the key to every measure of wealth, health & potential human happiness.

Where the cosmos seems to have 'willed' these relationships into a sustained existence, the path forward for humanity is clear. What the cosmos accomplished over billions of years, we must replicate in our lifetimes, as a means to the same success.

Where the cosmos 'will' created, with opportunity, the environment that could then emerge as life, humans need to understand the needed 'will' to realize such a correlative social reality as exists naturally in our bodies, can ONLY be realized if we link a true vision of human potential with an concerted & sustained effort that can move us beyond the inconveniences & challenges that already hold humanity in its thrall of continuity of human created harm.

When we finally accept the inevitability of the need for interpersonal relationships, of a particular moral quality & form, then we are on the path to the 1st rationality.

Maturity the behavioral indication of a skill of heartistic integration into beloved community, this then becomes the hallmark of human identity.

This integration of such values argues that we have recognized & accept the wisdom of the cosmos, as our 1st wisdom, the emerging evidence of a quality of choosing to care, that when supported as a cultural human habit, then becomes a nature, a species instinct.

The human instinct to co-create a sustainable beloved community, as the natural extension of the family into the greater social environment… is then the 'way of being' for all families.

The cosmos' wisdom then becomes our natural inheritance. Hence, our wisdom.

Then humans act rationally, because they grasped the 1st rational premise… the absolute need & value of relationships… to the human enterprise.

Once one assumes that 1st premise as the foundation for championing a true human value system, we end up at the door of the need to love… & to be loved, as the ONLY distinction that marks the human, as truly human.

There is no other truly human rationality.

Forgiveness & repentance: Forms of celebrating 'patriotism'

(Where two were divided, today, two choose to stand together...)

"Whom would take knee in repentance for harms created, offers no power to others, no honoring but to self, where the first betrayal occurred, hence, the first debt is to be paid."
The Last Spiritual Samurai

"If injustice is bad for the individual, it is not because it contradicts an eternal idea of justice, but because it perpetuates the silent hostility that separates the oppressor from the oppressed. It kills the small part of existence that can be realized on this earth through the mutual understanding of men. In the same way, the man who lies shuts himself off from other men, falsehood is therefore prescribed & on a slightly lower level, murder & violence, which impose definitive silence." Albert Camus

I have been led to believe that forgiveness & repentance are social skill sets generally not needed, EXCEPT IN EXTRAORDINARY CIRCUMSTANCES.

Hmm... you'll pardon me if I hold this ever so slightly disturbing to my sense of not only the social requirements for mere civility, I find it more critical to the very psychological health that is needed by individual or culture.

Yet, even more profoundly, such social skills are the root value orientation that EVERY true patriot has access to & rations as circumstances requires… not as convenience would offer.

The patriot is the citizen who understands that in articulating that "all are created equal,' a social contract is enacted that is intended 1st & foremost as a benefit… & a protection.

Hence, the 1st person needing our defense is our neighbor, for it is that person that signifies the social significance of those four fated words. THAT person is the 1st individual we know, beyond ourselves, that might be so affected as to need our intervention.

The citizen who assumes the mantle of patriot, of defender of the values of a nation, THAT individual then offers the values to the social arena that MOST FULLY OFFER THE POTENTIAL FOR HEALTHY, MORALLY SIGNIFICANT INTERPERSONAL RELATIONSHIS TO REACH THEIR PINNACLE OF MORAL POTENTIAL, IN CREATING NOT ONLY CIVILITY & COMMUNITY, BUT ALSO DEFINING THE NATURE OF THE INTEGRATED CIVILIZATION.

In this parade of characters, events & outcomes, all elements of morally significant relationships are attended; thus, from the unconditional love of parents as they offer to their 1st child, to the need for attending deviance, in the supporting role of forgiveness, to the final call for self-love revealed in repentance,, the values that inform community, that created beloved community, then are the tools of the citizen, as they interact with their environment. It is here that the patriot appears.

When I own my own deviance, whether such cognition & commitment comes from a social confrontation, or our own internal ongoing 'judgement day,' as an act of self-purification, we offer ourselves the greatest freedom imaginable. It is not about balancing an equation of this amount of wrong equals that amount of restorative offering. Rather, it is in the heart of seeking integration, in the corresponding offering, an offering of heart, of desire for relationship, that bridges the opportunity of the past harmed to a renewed opportunity to re-create, as a co-creation. Thus, the process begins… a process of time, effort, integration.

First of all, we are creating a socially significant shared reality. In this, we are also 'restoring' the past in the ONLY way that can be corrective. When it is corrective to the shared community & the psychological/spiritual states of those impacted, including the deviant themselves. We can't go back into history. But we can come to such a state of shared integration, that the 'now' we share becomes the 'all' we are concerned about. This is both the desire of the deviant who repents, it is also the very heart of the desire of those who truly seek to forgive.

To forgive is to surrender to the original desire & effort… beloved community. Be it a community for a minute or a lifetime, intimate or casual, to forgive is to celebrate the restoration of the relationship in the best way possible… as it always could, as we do. We 'celebrate' in that our purpose is beloved community & thus, co-creation.

Life on its most fundamental level is merely the sustained co-creation of morally significant sustainable relationships. Life thus is in each moment of cohesion & growth the affirmation of a potential of relationship, however far it may traverse in terms of all its potentials & the need for a supporting ecosystem & environment.

Hence, the human, in not acting in the natural accord of the cosmos, to participate in such morally significant social relationships as to contribute to the health & stability of a social system, can re-establish oneself by making such corrective actions as may restore a state of sustained community. The isolated entity, if its own nature has determined it is best served by community & integration in community, & acts as an anarchist, may discover the 'way of the Dodo".

There are two issues then at risk when we deviate. We offer to change ourselves in ways that we have not considered the long-term significance of. A juncture in the road we are following may seem close together as we separate, but the farther we travel our respective orientations, the less distinct we become to each other, until we neither recognize each other, nor do we appear same moral horizon.

Freedom vs anarchy: The call to greatness

(I am vs we are)

"Only a refusal to hate or kill can put an end to the chain of violence in the world & lead us toward a community where men can live together without fear. Our goal is to create beloved community & this will require a qualitative change in our souls as well as a qualitative change in our lives." M.L. King, Jr.

"There was never a moment in American history more honorable & more inspiring than the pilgrimage of clergymen

& laymen of every race & faith pouring into Selma to face danger at the side of its embattled Negroes." M.L. King, Jr.

"Our purpose is to find our whether innocence, the moment it becomes involved in action, can avoid committing murder. We can only act in terms of our own time, among the people who surround us. We shall know nothing until we know whether we have the right to kill our fellow men, or the right to let them be killed. In that every action today leads to murder, direct or indirect, we cannot act until we know whether or why we have the right to kill." Albert Camus

"If freedom is to be extended, it must discipline itself both personally & communally. On the personal level this means developing a unity of purpose so that choosing & action are harmonious for the self. This also involves a communal awareness & concern for the individual is part of society. Thus, unity has normative features in conjunction with freedom." John K Roth

"... the human race's irresistible urge to depart the path marked put by nature toward developing the capacities for goodness... thus made man himself unworthy of existing as a species designated to rule over the earth..." Immanuel Kant

The reality of life dictates, yes, life itself dictates the terms of life. What does that mean? There is no life without the corresponding elements that forge it & bring it into being. The number one point to note? The significance of elements in relationship to the development of life. Life itself, versus the elements that comprise its 'beingness', is a composite of sustainable interpersonal relationships, revealing further potentials.

Freedom in the cosmos is revealed in the events wherein something greater is created than the mere sum of the individual parts.

What are the elements needed for creation? The building blocks themselves. The internal & external resources needed in context of the potentials of the actors, individually & in concert. Then, each element offers its own natural potentials that can then be stimulated by the 'environment'. Proton & electron come together in such configurations as to create an atom. But the variety of potentials can, with the 'right' resources & ecological environment, stimulate unique developments. As each contributes the whole of its being to the new configuration of relationship(s). A simple proton & electron, in a chance encounter, bind their futures together. Their potentials that can be integrated... do.

Today... you have two eyes.

I have two eyes...

The potential revealed in the developing relationships & with support from the surrounding environment.

Why does the proton & electron have such an 'internal nature' so as to bond as opportunity & potential & environment might support?

Some observe that the 'material' of the cosmos is liken to being God's 'body'. Reflecting, in the organization of its forms as they move towards potentials of integration & 'community', the internal nature of the creator & creative force behind the scenes.

Yet, sourced by 'God' or some other phenomena not yet reasoned from the evidence, life exists in ONLY such sustainable relationships as we observe.

This observation offers one & ONLY one compelling argument. The very source of life, its sustainability, its uniqueness & diversity, its very tenacity, is all linked to the moral significance of the values that can not only create such relationships, but sustain them over time... & thus, through all the throes of environmental challenges than might occur, naturally or created.

Hence, the 'wisdom' of the cosmos, in the emergence of life, in its sustainability as well as its diversity, is in the moral significance of interpersonal values universally affecting all actors, incorporated in the very behavior of the actors.

The cosmos thus offers, in the 'wisdom' that was needed for life to emerge, that in such relational values is the key to life, to diversity, to 'prosperity' or life in abundance.

Here opportunity knocks at the door of human reason & reasoning.

Humans have a degree of 'freedom' unimaginable in any other species yet encountered. In the combination of 'freedoms', humanity has options not available anywhere else. Between our physical mobility, physical dexterity, rationality & our sense of self & being that exists multidimensionally, in the past, present & future, creating meaning unique to human experience, we have a degree of freedom that we have yet to understand, much less use in any sense exhibiting wisdom... much less genuine knowledge.

We live in hell.

We create hell each day.

We imagine how to create it for tomorrow.

Observe the pattern?

Twofold. We chose particular interpersonal values, expedient to only our own concerns, priorities & biases. We employ those values situationally. We participate on two levels of freedom. We 'chose,' unconsciously or not, the values to be employed… then, we chose to act.

But is the freedom to act REALLY THE VALUE AT ISSUE HERE… OR AT ANY TIME?

OR… IS THE ISSUE & HAS IT NOT ALWAYS BEEN THE ISSUE, WHAT WERE THE SOCIALLY SIGNIFICANT, MORALLY INFORMING & DEFINING INTERPERSONAL VALUES, CHOSEN TO BE APPLIED TO ANOTHER, WITH OR WITHOUT THEIR BLESSING?

Is our emphasis thus poorly placed?

When we observe all the harm created in history, are our uses of freedom & its value misplaced?

Is not the MOST VALUABLE HUMAN asset in all actuality, rather than merely the freedom to choose, it is in the capacity to choose the morally significant informing values themselves, that can then be applied to life & living, in imitation & replication of the success & wisdom of the cosmos, that then offers true prosperity?

Hence, if fully grasped for our consideration? What is unique to humanity is the opportunity for the form the values will take, that then will create life in the moment, as we act, alone & with each other.

Since all life & its diversity & prosperity is based upon such values naturally employed by the elements of life, then humans acting in such accord, to create our own form of life, the human species in its final perfection of refining its instinctual nature, then justifies its own freedom.

Why do I offer it 'justifies' its freedom & WHY would we have to?

Simple… remember the Dodo?

You don't? They're extinct.

They couldn't muster the ONLY choices that could sustain life.

Look around… look in the mirror.

We look more & more each day like the Dodo…

If nature is kind, it may allow us to completely commit species suicide. The final joke on the human understanding of the value & only proper use of freedom.

We may yet become the species that rendered a whole planet unlivable… uninhabitable.

Humanity's legacy… our unique gift.

Our form of gratitude.

Our freedom.

A question of wisdom & human maturity: Integration the innate relational nature of the cosmos

"Mother, mother
There's too many of you crying
Brother, brother, brother,
There's far too many of you dying
You know we've got to find a way
To bring some loving here today, yeah

Father, Father
We don't need to escalate
You see, war is not the answer
For only love can conquer hate
You know we've got to find a way
To bring some loving here today" Marvin Gaye

There is no more important issue before humanity than to discover the means to restrict, limit, guide or inform the human creature as the best & only means to create the truly civil family, the truly civil society… as the foundation to develop an international culture.

Yes, I just overheard the moans from those who think everything international means to demean one's own standing & also to open up to influences from such sources as communists.

Yet, under the daily witness to the onslaught & duress that humanity is forced to accept, as its daily fare, then some effort towards not just important knowledge is indicated & crucial, but instead, we need to set our sights a little higher, rather seeking some form of wisdom, if such is within the grasp of human minds & hearts.

But how will we recognize pertinent knowledge, much less wisdom?

If human maturity is measured in our sustainable social capacity for meaningful integration into community, then the global & individual state of humanity argues an evidence that suggests we are in dire straits. As such, while no one can force another to a sustained effort, we individually, in our families, churches & nations, have reached such a state of civil warfare that we don't even try to care anymore.

Recent elections in the US establish with the moral antipathy people have towards sustaining any meaningful integration, much less any true effort at honoring one another as worthy of the designation that "all are created equal" & thus have a natural obligation to one another to act as if so.

I monitored the various news outlets & was disturbed by my findings, however unscientific. There was sufficient bias in most news outlets that one was forced to filter the news or invest in the bias… or indulge it.

Trump-support based reporting offered the most extreme & sustained diatribe against the 'enemy'. It seemed about 70% of their 'reporting' was actually interpreted & prefiltered & developed narratives. Not only that, but the willful habit of intentionally repeating falsehoods, as if true, when already discredited, were constant behaviors. Pridefully so. The quality of personal & professional arrogance obvious in even the rhetorical patterns of speech & facial behavior was discouraging for the intentional bias it sought to generate/support. This offered as if actually representing a moral accounting of social events.

That the moral counterpart to Trump's news sources, though operating with much less bias & moral ineptitude & ambivalence than the Trump news sources, still fell prey to the temptation to go beyond reporting, to politicalizing events, is telling on the rational state of our values… in the public arena, where citizenship & patriotism are ultimately revealed.

The greater point missed in such indulgences is the tendency then to become the enemy in all the ways one sought to confront them. With the truth. Then, it is not that we become them, we ARE them.

When a major portion of the country neither cares that the president is essentially an evil person for the values that inform his every decision, & includes such an audience that cannot even intellectually determine why Trump is anti-American, anti-Jesus & anti-God, merely allows Trump to have a blank check.

Such lack of moral concern for the character of our nation's representative to the world is then also our statement of respect for that world & ITS people. Trump doesn't care about anyone except himself, hence, that message is not only communicated to those he takes offense to as an enemy, it also translates into impact on international relationships unilaterally, to enemy & ally, both personally & politically.

When such behaviors as revenge, even as rhetorical forms, are acted out on the international stage, it also impacts then the relationships of the nations; then populaces are held hostage to the mores, values & civil skills of the various actors, formal & those with power behind the scenes.

If one understands the individual, public & political social significance of a nation that establishes that 1st public & morally defining principle, that all are created equal, then one can also access rationally & grasp the indicated social significance of such a standard, to not only international discourse, but the very quality of effort made towards a true global community.

If all are created equal, my enemy no less than ANY other, then my social obligation to my own measure of my humanity, my standing as a citizen & my commitment to the innate patriotism that being human should inspire, then this social measure applies no less to the international community.

Our social & political maturity is then revealed for all to observe &/or experience. The 'heart' of our genuine desire for community is then the 'evidence' of behavior.

When we degrade our offerings to others, based upon personal, social or political concerns, justified in our hearts as not needing the conscience to direct us, we degrade ourselves. When my offering to you is insincere, when it is false, then I have disgraced myself, by lying to you about myself & how I really view myself.

"Caring? My offering reeks of it. Sincere? I spared no effort not warranted to move us into the sacred. To be trusted? I live with myself, either I live in hell or at peace. You will know. How do I thus value you? I offer you no less than I would offer myself."

A leader is first & foremost the moral rudder for the greater whole.

You don't care for the values informing the morality of your leader?

Then expect that where the rubber meets the road, you too, will be subject to the same valuation.

Expendable.

Now one can argue that this is within his 'right' to do. NO, IT IS NOT. THAT IT IS NOT ILLEGAL IS NOT THE SAME AS TO SAY IT HAS A NATURAL MORAL AUTHORITY THAT CANNOT BE PUBLICLY CHALLENGED.

That is the extreme hubris of the values that define Trump & those like him, that make up a substantial part of the American persona now indulged by our human populace.

What? So we not recognize ourselves to some degree in Trump & his cult? We are either not looking close enough or, more likely, not being honest. My suggestion? We come back another day. We will find it worth it in the end... & worthy of us for the self-definition we create.

Every witness to life we observe, offers the final proof as to the individual & social significance of relationships, & thus integration, as the moral witness to the values needed for life as a sustainable factor of existence. If freedom to choose were the highest tier interpersonal value, then the human body could not exist as a physical reality. It is ONLY in the sustained commitment, the fruit of some internal nature or decided by processes & proximity not yet fully understood, that the human eye can exist, in itself, & in its form & significance to its environment, with its innate ecology.

The wisdom of the cosmos stresses the innate value of relationships, for the 'moral' place they play in the very development of the possibility of life to emerge. Were not the foundational particles primed to the potential for relationships, either in direct potentials or as a result of an interplay of environmental factors, the bottom line is still the living 'evidence' of the personal & public significance posed by the engagement of relationship.

The implied wisdom for humanity, given the significance of freedom & individuality to humanity, then argues that some willful accommodation is naturally required of humanity to engage this wisdom for its own. Should this be such a surprising revelation?

The first natural benefactor to the social significance of an engaged moral accommodation to relationships is noted in the family. To create order between the various actors, adult & child. To prepare the child to also participate meaningfully, for the sake of self, family &, if indicated, a greater social environment.

If such relationships are the foundation for all other relationships, then the values informing such a social system becomes important on multi-dimensional levels of human concern. What is sacred, what is deviant, what is formal & what is casual, what is morally acceptable & what is not. Hence, not only the values chosen to inform such relationships is important, but to what standard as a sustained expectation of commitment, as a morally significant social norm, is also critical to the hoped-for outcomes.

The social reality of this world argues several points.

We DO understand the importance of integration.

We DO understand the personal, public & political potential posed by the possibility of healthy relationship.

We DO understand what unconditional love is... even of not as a sustained commitment.

We DO understand the value of forgiveness, even if not rationally, for the breadth & depth of relationship it can serve.

We DO understand the health of repentance, not only to re-enter sacred community, but to one's own psychological health, well-being & order in the universe.

We DO observe the significance of relationships, to life & living, even if it doesn't enter into the equation of our lives & living.

We do observe the fact that if one does not adapt to the demands of the environment one occupies, then extinction is as likely an outcome as any other imagined result. Note the DoDo…

Thus, as it ever was, what does life offer to us, as wisdom? How can we not only interpret that wisdom, how can we bridge the gap between genuine need & value & apathy & arrogance?

Got an answer?

Book 2

The universal sociological significance
of Jewish & American histories

Heaven moves history: "ALL... are created equal" as the 1ˢᵗ civil right

(Today I offer to you what was once denied me)

"... I provisionally defined morality as a science that teaches, not how we can be happy, but how we ought to become worthy of happiness." Immanuel Kant

"Analysis of rebellion leads at least to the suspicion that, contrary to the postulates of contemporary thought, a human nature does exist..." Albert Camus

"The spirit of rebellion can exist only in a society where a theoretical equality conceals factual inequalities." Albert Camus

"The slave who oppose his master is not concerned, let us note, with repudiating his master as a human being. He repudiates him as a master. He denies that he has the right to deny him, a slave, on the grounds of necessity. The master is discredited to the exact extent that he fails to respond to a demand which he ignores. If men cannot refer to a common value, recognized by all as existing in each one, then man is incomprehensible to man... The most elementary form of rebellion, paradoxically, expresses an aspiration to order." Albert Camus

"Now I say that man, & in general every rational being, exists as an end in himself & not merely as a means to be arbitrarily used by this or that will. He must in all his actions, whether directed to himself or to other rational beings, always be regarded at the same as an end... rational beings are called persons inasmuch as their nature already mark them out as ends in themselves... Such an end is one for which there can be substituted no other end to which such beings should serve merely as a means, for otherwise nothing of absolute value would be found anywhere... The practical imperative will therefore be the following" Act in such a way that your treat humanity, whether in your own person or in the person of another, always at the same time as an end & never simply as a means." Immanuel Kant

"No (wo)man is worth his/her salt who is not ready at all times to risk his/her body... to risk his/her well-being... to risk his/her life... in a great cause." Theodore Roosevelt

Human history as wisdom in our social/civil evolution: Abraham, Moses & Jesus

Intro...

"The purpose of this essay is once again to face the reality of the present, which is logical crime, & to examine meticulously the arguments by which it is justified; it is an attempt to understand the times in which we live." Albert Camus

"The attitude & ethos that distinguish the politics of a civil society is civility, i.e., a solicitude for the interest of the whole society, a concern for the common good. The civil person, when he has to decide & act in a situation in which there is conflict, thinks primarily of the civil society as the object of obligations, not of the members of his family, or his village, or his party, or his ethnic group, or his social class, or his occupation." Edward Schils

"Civility in private life & civility in the face-to-face relations of participants in public life are NOT essentially different from each other." Edward Schils

"...(citizenship) implies membership in a community defined by a common substantive end, more comprehensive, more dignified, more authoritative than the particular ends of private individuals." Clifford Orwin

"The established religions & their adherents have never realized that man has a central responsibility for turning this evil world around." Rev. S.M. Moon

"Here then is the origin & rise of government; namely a mode rendered necessary by the inability of moral virtue to govern the world..." Thomas Paine

"Fifth Thesis: The greatest problem for the human species, whose solution nature compels it to seek, is to achieve a universal *civil society* administered in accord with the right." Immanuel Kant

"Wherefore, security being the true design & end of government, it unanswerably follows that whatever *form* thereof appears most likely to ensure it to us, with the least expense & greatest benefit, is preferable to all others." Thomas Paine

"Primary among the resources available to the human quest are, of course, those features of its own nature that best equip it respond to the obstacles met in living. The advancement of these characteristics constitutes the evolutionary development of *homo sapiens*. If we can identify

these features, we will have located the evolutionary ground of moral value; for such attributes are valuable precisely because they are essential to the continuance & extension of humanity. An individual cannot aim his/her conduct at the survival of the species, but one CAN aim at nurturing those natural capacities upon which species survival depends."
Christopher Lyle Johnstone

"If injustice is bad for the individual, it is not because it contradicts an eternal idea of justice, but because it perpetuates the silent hostility that separates the oppressor from the oppressed. It kills the small part of existence that can be realized on this earth through the mutual understanding of men. In the same way, the man who lies shuts himself off from other men, falsehood is therefore prescribed & on a slightly lower level, murder & violence, which impose definitive silence." Albert Camus

"Only a refusal to hate or kill can put an end to the chain of violence in the world & lead us toward a community where men can live together without fear. Our goal is to create beloved community & this will require a qualitative change in our souls as well as a qualitative change in our lives." M.L. King, Jr.

"Our purpose is to find our whether innocence, the moment it becomes involved in action, can avoid committing murder. We can only act in terms of our own time, among the people who surround us. We shall know nothing until we know whether we have the right to kill our fellow men, or the right to let them be killed. In that every action today leads to murder, direct or indirect, we cannot act until we know whether or why we have the right to kill." Albert Camus

"If freedom is to be extended, it must discipline itself both personally & communally. On the personal level this means developing a unity of purpose so that choosing & action are harmonious for the self. This also involves a communal awareness & concern for the individual is part of society. Thus, unity has normative features in conjunction with freedom." John K Roth

"... the human race's irresistible urge to depart the path marked put by nature toward developing the capacities for goodness... thus made man himself unworthy of existing as a species designated to rule over the earth..." Immanuel Kant

"... I provisionally defined morality as a science that teaches, not how we can be happy, but how we ought to become worthy of happiness." Immanuel Kant

"Analysis of rebellion leads at least to the suspicion that, contrary to the postulates of contemporary thought, a human nature does exist..." Albert Camus

"The spirit of rebellion can exist only in a society where a theoretical equality conceals factual inequalities." Albert Camus

"The slave who oppose his master is not concerned, let us note, with repudiating his master as a human being. He repudiates him as a master. He denies that he has the right to deny him, a slave, on the grounds of necessity. The master is discredited to the exact extent that he fails to respond to a demand which he ignores. If men cannot refer to a common value, recognized by all as existing in each one, then man is incomprehensible to man... The most elementary form of rebellion, paradoxically, expresses an aspiration to order." Albert Camus

"Now I say that man, & in general every rational being, exists as an end in himself & not merely as a means to be arbitrarily used by this or that will. He must in all his actions, whether directed to himself or to other rational beings, always be regarded at the same as an end... rational beings are called persons inasmuch as their nature already mark them out as ends in themselves... Such an end is one for which there can be substituted no other end to which such beings should serve merely as a means, for otherwise nothing of absolute value would be found anywhere... The practical imperative will therefore be the following" Act in such a way that your treat humanity, whether in your own person or in the person of another, always at the same time as an end & never simply as a means." Immanuel Kant

"For God, to be a man, he must despair." Albert Camus

"Nature has willed that man, entirely by himself, produce everything that goes beyond the mechanical organization of his animal existence & partake in no other happiness or perfection than what he, himself, independently of instinct, can secure by his own reason." Immanuel Kant

"A creature's natural capacities are destined to develop completely & in conformity with their end." Immanuel Kant

"The greatest problem for the human species, whose solution nature compels it to seek, is to achieve a universal civil-society administered in accord with the right." Immanuel Kant

"Surely it is permissible *to insert* speculations in the *progression* of a history in order to fil out the gapes in the reports, because what comes before as distant cause, &

what follows, as effect, can give a fairly reliable clue for discovering the intervening causes as to make the transition comprehensible.: Immanuel Kant

In the greater context of the moral & social development of humanity, as individuals & as groupings of individuals, each of the above quotes is terribly important to understanding the challenges we have faced in history, the questions needing answering, the suffering that must now be justified rationally.

To some degree, with some success, our rationality & our capacity to care has given us such pause as to offer the potential wisdom as noted in the offered reflections. I note it is actually only potential wisdom, for wisdom to truly be qualified for such a distinguishment, we must accept its then need to be utilized... or it remains merely a potential.

Human social evolution is in all actuality the record of the human rational realization of the value & importance of not only relationships, but relationships of a particular moral tapestry, one flattering to integration & sustainable community.

The nature of the realization is that for any form of community to exist, there needs to be established a basis for trust & cohesion. There needs to be a form of covenant... a reconning of interpersonally significant values & thus, expected social behaviors. The harms of human history, experienced as a staple universally, has naturally given rise not only to issues of rebellion & protests, but such a serious reflection on the issue, as a universal human issue, that we discover thinkers from all recorded eras offered some thinking on the progress of civilization & its challenges. Force may have been the means to power, but even there, reasoning was the greatest aid to such effort.

If reasoning serves the madman with the same passion & abandonment that brings domination & subjugation as a reasoned means to an end, then reasoning might offer that an equivalent effort made in defense of a humanity yet free from living terrorism might in time yield fruit equal to the task imagined.

This is the world that humanity encounters, sans the religious interpretations that are added to events as being the resident causes & influencers. All humanity suffers the same needs for relationships, hence, the need for civilization... for civility.

Once we cross the threshold of civility, we encounter the social creation of 'morality.' When two individuals need community, for a minute or a lifetime, with such reasoning capacities as humans exhibit, then what kind of considerations must now be offered as critical mass to the purpose at hand?

We need good judgement... we need wisdom.

As mentioned earlier, social scientists have now identified & labeled what they refer to as the dark side of human nature.

I think a more appropriate interpretation is that the 'dark side' of human nature are merely the anti-social values of the anti-social personality, realized in such prioritizing of oneself, to oneself & the world in equal measure, as to create the ultimate measure of the moral foundations for identifying deviance.

A deviance that is admittedly biased... but only as ultimately the cosmos must be. Or suffer the fate of the Dodo. Extinction.

The counter to such values?

The family.

But a sociologically evolved family. One that has recognized the needs for a civility, a means of establishing such interpersonal priorities, that a social order is created, imagined to serve the whole, in meeting the needs of the parts. In moral proportion to need & resources.

There is little evidence to reveal the general & regional forms of moral compasses that developed in families, except as noted histories of important cities/states might reveal, that outlasted the fall of such societies.

To care... the rational act of assigning such interpersonally significant 'value' to something or someone, so as to radicalize the perception of a need of attendance & investment as to create an exclusivity of beingness.

While much ado has been made about the natural & unnatural emotional associations & displays that may merge in the context of a realized significant relationship, that one 'cares,' it is also not to be ignored that deviance often involves its own corresponding range of emotional experiences. The flavor of such experiences the same shades of bias that contribute to the harms associated with sadism. The pleasure of inflicting harm or in its observance.

The roots of civil behavior, as a morally significant sociological statement for religious communities has risen at various times, in many forms.

But the Judaic/Christian tradition as evidence of a natural & recognizable social pattern of moral commitment to civility is of particular interest to us.

For the tradition of civility & social intercourse that became 1st 'being Jewish' & also evolved, or devolved as one interprets, into much of what is now Judaic/Christian terms of civility, offers a social accessible & observable moral development.

With the emergence of a 'God' entity that sought relationship with humanity, the discourse about the purpose or destiny of humanity, as a particular group or species, was elevated to where men could now even be the offspring of Gods intercourse with the human race.

Humanity had aspirations to 'be more' that it was… grander, more in control of life & its forces, the victimizer, not the victim. The hero, the savior, the mentor, guide & messiah emerge as the sages who will intervene with such wisdom, be it force of arms or ideas, but humanity WILL BE SAVED.

Saved… not salvaged.

That came with Christianity.

With Abraham, a whole new quality of relationship was imagined. One that required a new quality of investment of intent, of purpose & thus, rationality & reasoning. The focus was on developing such patterns of intercourse that every effort was made to treat & honor God not only in such fashion as his station demanded, but also to create traditions of intercourse & attendance that would offer that seriousness at which humanity attended it now implied duties.

But duties not intended for servants, as was imagined. But rather acting as a social agent seeking to advance the cognitive awareness of not only the potential of relationships, but offering in such attendance & offering, a sustained state of individual & community 'care' as to revolutionize the imagination as to the potential to multiply such values beyond its immediate employment. The 'hint'? God cared about humanity enough to initiate relationship, but also to instruct on how to properly attend those relationships we must 'honor', or care about, & how much to care about such efforts & offerings.

The point?

Humanity 'matters' to God; God also desires humanity cares about God.

But how much are we to care…about God or how much does God care about us? That answer begins to emerge in the perception of God's integration into the affairs of humanity. God seems to take sides, to have now a favorite. But a favoritism that is sustained in a behavioral offering equated then as evidence of a sustained & honored faith in the covenant.

The covenant in reality… "when you grow up, you will 'inherit' as your portion of our journey…"

We will, in a contextually guided reflection, realize just how apropos an observation that is.

The 1st social emergence of a universal standard of social civility, or even regional civility, that held the sacred value of not only the individual, but operated as a co-created social system of integrated individuals, that system of specific values implied & associated with the standard for defining 'citizenship', or co-created community, became the creation of the Jewish estate.

With Abraham, a course leading to a generalized social civility was created, to 'honor' those whose perceived social value demanded exceptional attendance. This would be recognized as the respect or deference given parents, elders, servants, (yes, even & especially servants), managers & other supervisory roles, all mimicking the authority now associated with God... or parents.

Politics was born also.

The art of negotiating with authority... or other perceived centers of power. Power being the capacity to create 'effect' on others, to their benefit... or detriment.

Then, a revolution in social civility was effected with a 'nation' of peoples... or what would one day emerge to assume nationally defensible borders. Moses came into a position of leadership.

The dawn of a national socialization of the nature of the civility to be shared by a designated people emerged. The dawn of a new sense of identity, value & purpose, would be morally circumcised to a new standard of social sacredness.

Where once God was not indicated as to be interested in the internal & interpersonal affairs of the people was now indicated to have been amended. Now, we were to 'care' about God, to care about our individual & collective relationship with God. But also attached to this expression of the evolution of relationship with God, now we were also not to entertain certain behaviors, for the harm they force upon their victims.

NOW WE WERE ALSO TO CARE ABOUT EACH OTHER... DO NO HARM.

This is the rhetorical position & admonishment of a parent.

This quality of implied care was not recognized. There were no 'true' parents to have 'raised' their children with that needed standard. God as parent was still a ways off. Even so, with Moses, the people were further socialized to the value & purpose of relationships, based upon the avowed need & attendance to relationships with the moral sensibility to protect & honor the 'other' no less than ourselves.

Do not harm your neighbor by lying, stealing, killing, etc, offers only one message. "You ALL are important to me, & I desire you offer that same attendance to one another." The idea of civility now emerged as a means to define oneself to all others. Sharing that civility created its first citizens. Those who took it fully to heart became the 1st 'patriots'. The 1st line of defenders of the values of the people.

This was also the foundational event to outline the values needed to define the heart of every 'true parent'. With Moses, True Family Values were introduced by God. What are true family values?

Simply, true family values are the core base from which we have defined the world to us, in its moral significance. A significance ONLY revealed in behavior. Since the beginning, with Abraham, faith 'in God' was measured by the offering one sustained in behavior. This was our offering of faith being with God. Our behavior, our walk with God.

'True Family Values'
+ emerge in the unconditional heart of attendance offered in sustained behavior, with spouse, with children. Thus, as children learn the 'rules of the road' of community, of family, the social patterns for integration & social civility are established, as flesh & bones the 'way of life & living.'

This insures children learn the fullest meaning of repentance; repentance being the behavioral acts of contrition offered to re-establish the foundation for 'beloved community' to be restored & created.

True family values as the unconditional commitment to relationship, as the purpose & means to human fulfillment, both as a social exercise in life fulfillment but also as the means to the physical establishment of civility & civilization. Hence, forgiveness as the social extension of that commitment; repentance the culminating celebration of life brought to the restoration of deviance.

Into this scenario is only room for one hope... to establish the final standard to measure 'human love,' as a child of God... not as a servant.

This was the 'answer' Jesus offered, it was both the social solution to human created problems, it was also the means to the very intimacy & idealization of potential the people had held for God.

Jesus offered THE ONLY RATIONAL CONCLUSION TO THE CHALLENGES CREATED IN THE NATURE OF

THE INFORMING VALUES & THEIR RELATIONSHIP TO OUR UNDISCIPLINED USE OF FREEDOM WE ALLOWED OUR EMOTIONS OVER OUR CONSCIENCE, THE SOCIAL EXPRESSION OF OUR COMMITMENT TO CARE, THE CORE & HEART OF OUR BEINGNESS.

Jesus wisely offered that the nature of God's attendance had been in the nature of the heart offered, as a sustained effort. God eternally seeking communion & thus, community with humanity.

To be best understood by humanity in the image of a parent, for the nature of the attendance offered. Step by step offering the same moral, & thus loving content needed to not only socialize children to the need & value of certain qualities of relationships, but rather to so imprint them in this love that they naturally emerge as citizen/patriots.

This is the birth of Parentism as a social phenomena.

This is the social perfection of civility Jesus imagines is not only the potential of humanity, it also serves as the witness of our behavioral commitment to the co-creation of beloved community, be it for a moment, or for a life time. Jesus ONLY stipulation that established his remarkable life, for the witness to the choices HE HAD MADE, that it must be that we also bring our enemy home with us. For if we truly love God, then we would naturally love whom God would love, as God would love.

That is the simple yet profound 'wisdom' that emerged within the lives of a 'chosen' people… but no more or less chosen than the least of us, born or yet to come.

Simple formula for success… love your enemy no less than any other, hence, establishing the 'fact' that ALL are created equal, in the freedom we release each other to, in the love offered… & the love embraced.

We should be grateful…

In the inheritance of the opportunities & values that can inform our civility, to define our humanity, we become 'perfect as our father/parent', we thus offering our enemy the keys to their own freedom.

IN THIS, WISDOM IS BORN, WISDOM IS CO-CREATED… WISDOM IS REVEALED.

Israel & America: The 'moral man' in the development of civil history

(Observing oneself in the mirror of time)

"...we've come here today to dramatize a shameful condition. In a sense, we've come to our nation's capital to cash a check. When the architects of our republic wrote the magnificent words of the Constitution & the Declaration of Independence, they were signing a promissory note to which every American was to fall heir." M.L. King, Jr.

"I believe that unarmed truth & unconditional love will have the final word in reality." M.L. King, Jr.

"The logic of the rebel is to want to serve justice so as not to add to the injustice of the human condition, to insist on plain language so as not to increase the universal falsehood, & to wager, in spite of human misery, for happiness." Albert Camus

"A philosophical attempt to work out a universal history of the world in accord with a plan of nature that aims at a perfect civic union of the human species must be regarded as possible & even helpful to this objective of nature's." Immanuel Kant

In the revolutionary treatise, *The ONLY Possible God,* is provided a unique interpretation of Jewish history. I offer that history, specifically Jewish history, provides a sociologically & rationally accessible pattern that requires definition & interpretation.

It is not just the 'fact' that this history speaks to a pattern specifically as its uniqueness. The pattern itself spans millennia, is focused on three primary actors, is progressive & cumulative in nature, 'coincidences not easily explained away.

The pattern demands interpretation… but in doing so, a conundrum is created. There are, rationally speaking, two potential interpretations to these events. One is allowed in its native religious interpretation, not just as a matter of some kind of 'fairness' but rather because the 'effect' naturally 'sought' in such experiences is both 'natural' to human experience, a rational secular interpretation of the same history renders EXACTLY the same moral interpretation of its sociological significance & as a moral lesson for all of humanity.

Jewish history is the record of the natural socialization of humanity into a civil creature. Religious interpretation, or rational interpretation, Jewish history reveals the pattern experienced in EVERY family, in its essence, in the process of preparing children to assume their roles as citizens… & if prepared wholly, to become citizen/patriots, those whose every action is the actualization of the values of the nation.

Remarkably, in Jewish history, the citizen/patriot is created in the assumed nature of the values informing both the social civility of being Jewish, the moral nature of the covenant demanded in the amending values given Moses, but also it defines what it MUST mean TO BE HUMAN.

To be a 'good' Jew is thus to 'be Jewish' with all other Jews. In the nature of the trusted civility that is co-created, in the community that is created, the human being, being human, is given social definition & educational meaning for parenting.

Hence, to be a good Jew, was to be a good Jew with others, acting Jewish. Acting Jewish thus meant we were acting as 'God's' children. Thus, we were also 'being' human in the way God was indicated as seeking from humanity, the moral nature of God's activity now rationally accessible. The conclusion, in the values that guide all interpersonal integration, that to be Jewish was thus also 'to be human,' for the civility it not only creates, but offers is now as sustainable. This creates not only a culture. BUT SUCH VALUES ARE THE WELL-SPRING FOR THE RATIONAL EMERGENCE OF THE UNDERSTANDING OF WHAT TRUE FAMILY VALUES ARE. AS A UNIVERSAL VALUE ORIENTATION.

To choose to love is a rational act.

Possibly the 1st defining act of defining our own unique humanity.

To love is to offer, to surrender.

That is the witness of God in Jewish history.

That is the witness of the moral social evolution of the human species, as it matures in its understanding of the nature of life & its sustainable development.

In Jewish history, the evidence of a needed civility & the natural means to such a social state is revealed.

We must choose to care… whether we seek to please a God, sustaining our own offering of faith to that relationship, or we merely seek, in our own lives, the same success the cosmos had in creating life, sustainable life, hence… community. An ecologically natural environment of entities, existing in a state of integration.

Yet, Jesus, a Jew, argues & history now supports him, that the full intended relationship now only was NOT fulfilled as it was both willed by God, but also as it was socially supported by God to become a social reality.

Jesus offered that the completion of the covenant established with Abraham, was within the grasp of EVERY Jew… the promised kingdom of heaven was now on the horizon. But it required that last piece of the puzzle…what EXACTLY KEPT US IN THE HELL WE EXIST IN?

Jesus offered but one solution… Commit as a true parent would commit, forgiving as the force of our love translated as needed, to still be of service to the needs for community. God sustained the effort as civilizing humanity, amending the nature of the relationship first with Moses.

This foundational paradigm the core for establishing any healthy family no less than a nation. Love your parents, love your children, even when your children deviate & cause harm. Then, acting in proportion to the offense, always with the heart that desires integration, hence, restoration. Offering as is contextually significant to re-establishing community. Behaviorally revealing restoration & celebration... of relationship.

With the death of Jesus, & the failure of humanity to understand the thrust of human history, the Jewish people could not fully grasp the means needed to realize the fullness God sought, not just with God, but as the cumulative social reality of humanity, with one another.

The 'promised' kingdom of heaven.

Thus, THAT potential social global evolutionary opportunity, while still existing for any person who truly sought to understand Jesus & thus, offer the quality of faith Jesus demanded, no longer was the social nor internal focus of those seeking to multiply Christianity.

It was no longer about Jesus... it was about 'feeling good'. Lots of 'Christians, little of the evidence of Jesus.

Hence, the emergence of America. The priming of the 2nd Israel. But to what effect? For what purpose?

To establish not only the ONLY means to a true civility, but also to accept true civility is ONLY created when humanity accepts some morally significant interpersonal paradigm for social engagement with one another. Requiring a quality of informing values to promote civility that fulfills the potential & need of humanity, not only to establish community but also such a true state of such social civility that the suffering of history is no longer the norm.

But, the nation that could understand that final chasm refused to listen to one of its own sons. Jesus had the ONLY viable HUMAN ACCESSIBLE SOLUTION. Now, God needed another nation to lead to the final conclusion... when we not only establish true children of God, in the maturity of the values we now assume responsibility for, but we need true parents that can then naturally socialize the next generation, not to just emerge as citizens, but will be so committed in their own way of being that they then also become natural patriots, also defending a global potential for community. But that train had not yet entered the station. Jewish faith fell short in its understanding of the 'heart' of God.

Still, to be Jewish, was to be in a natural communion with every other Jew. Every child was naturally primed since childhood to find identity, security, community & stability in every encounter with every other Jew, globally. It was the humanity of civility co-created that justified that exceptional commitment. Family is as family does.

With the emergence of America, the lesson of civility & care that a people can bring to bear upon one another had been understood. The founders were not just struggling with a moment in time, they were confronting the fruits of history.

Intuitively, wisely or blindly, four words enshrined for the coming nation the ONLY value orientation that would naturally encourage the self-examination of one's behavior, as for its moral content & social impact. How to bind one to the other was needed… or anarchy would reign just as surely as it always had. How to inhibit while also freeing.

Offer such an identity, that one's own value is intrinsically not only bound to one's neighbor, one must come to feel & experience a natural benefit in the choice. If I seek my sense of freedom, & if my neighbor also shares the same essential desire, then the most perfect way to protect one's own interest will be in the affirmation of the other & in sharing a common commitment to support such community that both share in the fruits of its creation. This will come through social affirmation with others; it is also secured in our own being as hope, as our own social action that also affirms us, as experience is always one to do.

Where Mosaic Law called the people to a common commitment & social conscience, the American founders called upon her people to honor each other as equal, thus forcing a cognitive awareness of a new covenant was being established, on the authority of men to decide for humanity the only moral course ahead, one that restores history, in the creation of a new quality of life experience.

Further, in the effort to decide upon a means to honor all others as equal to oneself, the 1st realization will be in the engagement & integration of the Bill of Rights into the social conscious. Thus, if I am to honor your right to freedom of speech, then my engagement itself must morally allow for differences of view & thus, the need of such moral options as to allow for disagreement, without entertaining such values as to be willing to sacrifice the relationship, for the sake of dominating the environment.

The American sense of moral obligation is the same ANY potential community faces & must define. With the demand for a social consciousness & social conscience that ALWAYS seeks for community, if not consensus, then humanity is morally positioned to use human freedom in the ONLY way that is truly human… to choose to care.

That we are all created equal, reasoned by men or accepted as divine apportion, requires we consider the social significance of that fact, especially in light of both the need & benefit of such relationships.

Simply stated, to honor others in such fashion is to act with love. Even if the emotional experience is not a high five moment in every opportunity, emotions are a situational response of the body for significant events, not ultimately offering the same quality of sense of value we experience as we meaningfully integrate with each other & created beloved community. This as a sustained state.

With America, the 'moral man' met himself again in history. The moral man emerges in the freedom accepted & employed ONLY as humanity can… in the moral creation of our own true instinct & human nature. A nature that mimics the very success of the cosmos.

Once again, we were perfectly positioned to act with wisdom.

We bumped true freedom out of bed, rather opting for profit… over others. We treated the newly liberated freedom to be like a virtuous woman now paraded as a whore. With slavery, Americans institutionalized the perfect denial of that founding principle.

The ONLY saving grace?

The Amendment process.

The ONLY means to achieve a national level of needed repentance, even if the heart of most of the people were NOT in it. This was & is the ONLY way to indemnify the past... by creating a new now, that then offers the perfect judgement on that past, by offering its moral restorational substantial repentance, offered now in restored social behavior. The repentance of transforming the self, by transcending those previous values.

In all of this, even with the continuing failure of Americans to fully invest ourselves in 'being American,' the promise of the potential of America remains.

But it is the heart of a patriot that observes history, observes those words, observes the world & its families... & then chooses a value, never to waver again.

Civilization is created.

Book

3

The emperor & his court wear no clothes: The heresy that is America

That Illusive American Dream: It ain't about a Cadillac in every Black garage

"History reveals two qualities of rebels to history. Those that seek to be a benefit to the world, including to their enemy, in their own offering, & those who seek to re-imagine & re-create the world, but without their enemy, as a result of assuming the right to eliminate the enemy. This, rather than to integrate with the enemy, as an act of community creation & social & historical restoration." The Last Spiritual Samurai

I must admit to having become very confused of late. It was inevitable. Humanity, but specifically Americans, imagine a world where THEY are to dominate, where THEY are the entitled. Where THEY hit the lotto. When THAT doesn't happen, in time, we have a Trump who emerges, that cajoles the people into thinking HE represents their interests, their values. As HE exploits them for everything he can, appealing to emotions, he creates a new narrative, a new story. He is the hero, they the lady in distress. He speaks to them, for them, informing & articulating their needs, hurts & betrayals, real & imagined. He offers relief. He offers representation. He offers them identity. HE SEEMS TO CARE WHEN NO ONE ELSE DOES. Hence, the hope for relief. But recognition if nothing else. Sometimes a shout out is much more than a mere shout out. Sometimes a shout out is erringly interpreted also as a promise.

The promise then the nourishment in lieu of substantiation. But hope then is nurtured & natured.

Then, through this vehicle, the voice of a people may be imagined to be heard, & heard, acted upon with all due respect.

But to what hope, to what imagined promise broken? To what betrayal have such people become victims? Have they actually & fully identified the 'guilt' elements to their perceived & self-reported suffering? Or are they victims of a developing history for which they cannot either understand their role, much less their opportunities... or even if ANY kind or quality of guarantee exists for Americans?

When we fully engage the history that produced the human necessity for such a country to emerge, articulating & defining & defending the freedoms & values she does, America emerges as a nation existing for the sake of the world, not just a nation created for itself.

Why does America exist for the sake of the world?

Because she articulates, defines & defends the values & behaviors that have been denied in history, to humanity, for humanity.

Yet, if considered contextually, we must ask what value is MOST significant to America... & MOST SIGNIFICANT TO THE EXPERIENCE OF BEING AN AMERICAN. ESTABLISHING THAT SPECIFIC VALUE ORIENTATION, UNIVERSAL IN ITS APPLICATION, ITSELF ESTABLISHING A SOCIALLY SIGNIFICANT FORM OF AN ENDURING SENSE OF CO-CREATED NATIONAL EXCEPTIONALISM.

BEING an American offers one a sense of inherently that one is not only worthy, but this worthiness MUST be allowed & engaged as an equal to any other. By any other.

YET THAT VERY EXCEPTIONALISM THAT IS CREATED IN FOUR SIMPLE WORDS, OFFERS A

UNIVERSAL PARADIGM MUST BE ALLOWED, IF ONE IS TO ENGAGE THE VALUE ITSELF AT ALL. ONE'S OWN CLAIM IS ONLY SUBTANTIATED WHEN A COMMUNITY OF SUCH INDIVIDUALS OFFER TO EACH OTHER THE SUSTAINED MORALLY SIGNIFICANT ENVIRONMENT WHEREIN SUCH A COMMUNITY OF SACRED INDIVIDUALS COULD NOT JUST CO-EXIST BUT INTEGRATE SO AS TO CO-CREATE 'BELOVED COMMUNITY'.

It is ONLY in such a social climate & established environment, that the ecology of the social system can be of value to the least to need or desire to utilize it as to the most needing its support, such as the youngest & the elderly.

What 4 words did for America, God did for the Jews with the inception of the 10 Words given to Moses. Offering a universal moral center that it not only embraces the least, it offers the ONLY moral course for creating such a sustainable culture that a truly civil society can emerge, that embraces the most diverse forms of communities.

'God' demanded the Jewish people reconsider the nature of the moral compass they employed with one another, God offering that a greater form of morally significant community was now sought. A social entity wherein the harms created are now addressed as beyond the scope of the will of God, for the actor & the harmed. That the Jewish people did not truly grasp the social & moral significance of the effort of God through Moses, in their subsequent creation of such a burden of laws, that the internal hope & opportunity posed in the moral compass God offered Moses was not understood in the heart of the people, rather was anchored in a "MUST" universe that offers a punitive response for failure. This was NOT the true nature of the intervention initiated by God. Considered contextually, Jewish history offers that God was integrating with humanity in the same form & with the same values any truly loving parent would engage naturally.

Hence, in this scenario, God is seeking to liberate the individual, but a liberation that is ONLY realized in community with others. This establishing a 'family' of God, realized in a life of faith that is manifest in the nature of the values informing interpersonal relationships. Informed in the behaviors of the people, behavior the public measure of heart…

With the failure of the Jewish people to fully grasp the social significance of their own history, a feat no culture has achieved as yet, Jesus passed into history as a rebel, one offering some 'salvation', a salvation merely requiring a public declaration of filial piety to the 'blood' of Jesus.

Hence, with Christianity itself, as it socially evolved, it became a religion that has worshipped death, delivered death & in general, not been the vehicle for Jesus' true message & public mission. Christianity became the 1st international, profit centered, capitalistic enterprise. Christianity became the prototype for economic measures of social success, measured in the power one wields, to other's benefit… or to their detriment.

Failing to understand the true heart of Jesus, thus also never truly understanding the heart of their parent God, Christians could not avoid the pitfalls of success it naturally poses.

Where Jesus avoided all the temptations of 'Satan' as Satan honored Jesus for the social significance he was to come to witness to in behavior, Christian leaders learned the ways & means of public power, now marshalled in such form as to offer new avenues to wealth, however measured. Hence, in time, in the uses of power, in the indulgences allowed, taken & flaunted or denied or hidden, the Christian Church served itself much more than it served its God.

Yet, buried in the 'word of God' still remained the wealth of nations that Jesus had bestowed upon humanity originally, as our greatest gift, but also representing our greatest need.

Jesus understood that the whole of God's effort in history, from the beginning, had been to re-establish community... true love community with humanity, all of humanity, to the last & least. True love 'family'. When this simple factor is understood rationally, & then when we match that understanding with a clear grasp of the greatest human challenge, then we discover that Jesus offered EXACTLY THE VERY VALUES NEEDED TO FIND OUR WAY FORWARD... TO GOD, BUT BY WAY OF EACH OTHER, NO LESS OUR ENEMY THAN ANY OTHER.

What Jesus established was the moral paradigm needed to establish the foundation for a morally significant sustainable community. ANY community... A Muslim community. An atheistic community...or even a Christian community... or a Hindu community. Or even a marriage.

In other words, Jesus, when understood contextually, as history & human need defines & defends him, Jesus offers the tools needed to move past the history of humanity measured in unearned & unneeded suffering.

Jesus informed the Jews as to what is now, in retrospect, the ONLY values needed to address all human need as it emerged in the encounter with one another. But the missing element then, as it is now, is two-fold. Rational understanding & the unemotional & rational application of a determined human will, of the quality that allows no defeat, no loss of self to some outside force or unprincipled values.

Jesus informed us, in living example & word, the values that defined & informed the true child of God... hence, the truly human. Given the significance of such interpersonal relationships to the emergence of life & its sustainability, humanity is obviously challenged in this arena of cosmic meaning. With the values that Jewish history, God & Jesus offered as the means to full relationship with God, vis a vis each other, no less our enemy than any other, humanity was & is ONLY limited by our own investment towards a total understanding & corresponding needed effort.

When Israel rejected Jesus in the role & social significance he offered in the words & acts he offered were MOST human, MOST like the children of God, it was to the Christians to be the legend bearers, the standard bearers, the protectors of the word.

THAT DID NOT HAPPEN.

But then America emerged… inspired by the past, recent & the tortured past of humanity, an opportunity was created, a moment in time stopped to give humanity a chance to reflect on what it means to be human… in community, but a community composed of a sacred group of individuals.

The 10 Words given Moses established a sacred community of individuals, BUT ONLY REALIZED IN THE LIVING OF THE VALUES THAT WOULD NOT JUST INHIBIT INTERPERSONAL HARM, IT WOULD INSPIRE A DESIRE NOT TO HARM. ONLY in a community of equal individuals, which Moses tablets established naturally, could humanity hope to find a way out of the pattern of history that created such a sustained universal experience of human imposed suffering.

When Israel lost its way, as the leading civil society that could have realized the potential humanity has to reason its problem to a profitable solution, but for all of humanity, the Jewish nation the original seed, humanity was adrift. Israel the national level seed, like Jesus was the 1st Jewish individual seed. The 1st fully human seed.

There is no disputing the personal, public & political significance of the values the Jewish people offered, as they were offered. Love is a rational commitment 1st. The emotional support for the decision will emerge more situationally, whereas the root or core commitment is from the heart, the desire to care that allows for no distraction, no adulteration. That desire is a nurtured & natured desire, realized both in the quality of experiences we are exposed to & the moral alternatives available to be engaged. But to love is as a willed choice; a reasoned choice for the demands we place upon ourselves, not as a burden, but a joy yet to be explored for all the avenues of opportunity life will naturally expose us to.

With the birth of America, guided by the ONLY 4 words that equaled the 10 Words given Moses, Americans were not only 'promised' a land where freedom would have a meaning not the norm in the world, even to this day, but a land wherein freedom was shared in such form as to establish each person as a unique value to not only themselves, but this to be shared with all others… native or not. Hence, the daily fare would be a personal, public & political experience of not only equality, but experiencing the unique expressions of such shared civility with all others.

America offered the opportunity… 4 words defined & declared the values to be employed, the honor to be bestowed upon one another, freedom… the foundation for will, the only needed personal, public & political component NEEDED TO BE OFFERED BY EACH & EVERY ONE, TO EACH & EVERY OTHER. EVEN THE NON-CITIZEN… OR ENEMY. The will to the values of a nation, defending individuals as no nation since Israel had with Moses & Jesus, America would produce the 1st universal citizen/patriots. Patriots defined & defended in the living of the defined & defended values, even with our enemies.

But values are only articulated & defended when they are lived... THAT is the voice of witness, of evidence. Of reality.

America created a participatory opportunity to co-create what had never before truly yet existed. A nation of the people, for the people, by the people, but defined & morally guided by the only values that when employed with the heart of will, produces the quality of civility that we associate with beloved community... family.

But, like with Israel, a national level family, ONLY ESTABLISHED IN THE VALUES THAT INITIATE A SUSTAINABLE INTEGRATION... OF THE HEART, MIND & BODY.

The PROMISE of America, is the DREAM OF HISTORY... A FINAL TRUE HOME FOR HUMANITY. A home where...family is. Family as Jesus offered, a family realized in the values that create such relationships that no challenge is too great for our effort to realize them. Hence, we commit as a parent would, unconditionally. We forgive because it represents our continued commitment to love, to restore all opportunity for community, even in the experience of harms from deviance, willed or unintended. We repent because we seek to be whole, to also share in the ONLY quality of freedom that expresses true human potential. The freedom to so care, that even our failings become a source of cause for re-establishing community. Rather than a burden, freedom to repent is a means to self-love not realizable any other way.

America DEMANDS WE HONOR EACH OTHER AS EQUAL... THAT EACH MAY ALSO HAVE SUCH ACCESS TO ALL THE DEFINED, DEFENDED & IMPLIED FREEDOMS, SO THAT WE CAN ALL FULLY ACT AS TO REALIZE NOT ONLY OUR UNIQUENESS, BUT DISCOVER SUCH SOCIALLY SIGNIFICANT WAYS TO SHARE OURSELVES WITH OUR ENVIRONMENT THAT

WE NATURALLY EMERGE AS AN ASSET TO ANY COMMUNITY WE SEEK TO SHARE IN.

America's promise… AMERICA'S DREAM, IS A NATION, A HOME, A FAMILY, WHERE WE ARE EACH SO TREASURED, AS TO BE NATURALLY PROTECTED & ENCOURAGED TO EXPLORE & BE ALL WE CAN BE…

But with the Christian influx of an economic system of social exploitation, namely a church created & supported by a sense of entitlement & manifest destiny, creating a universal & global capitalism, the philosophy of an entitlement to profit justified merely by its success, not a moral founding & guiding principle as its core, the sacred value of the individual was redefined. But even this failure was defended & precipitated by the imagined entitlement that was revealed in slavery, as Christians failed here to honor those 1st four words. This would not bode well for America.

Now, white America would one day have to face judgment day… not a religious judgment day, but a social one. In the engagement of slavery, Americans accused themselves of the same 'sins' they had used rationally to justify their rebellion as righteous, & thus, under the auspices of heaven's protection & blessing. But the conscience was not allowed it true lead, the place in the heart that then controls those emotionally held values & biases that do not create community, nor sustain it, nor advance its interests. 4 words demanded the honor the nation required, to be a nation that could fulfill a true dream of humanity… THE FREEDOM TO BE HUMAN.

But a slave owner is not truly human…not by any measure we should want to sustain as a human nature, a human worthy value, to be carried forth in the thoughts, hearts & behaviors of the next generation, the torch bearers of the future of social civility. This nation provided a means to promote, protect & encourage an ongoing development of our social conscience, the educated tool & resource that holds the values we at least imagine we should honor, to love ourselves, much less anyone else.

Hence, ONLY with the end of slavery were Americans as a community back on course to evolve further along the line of reasoning 4 words sought to impact us with. That our own security lies in the hands of our neighbor. We, also of such social significance, that we are the last defense of our neighbor, against the ravages of history, that left victims & no other justification than the remaining hearts, minds & bodies that litter history.

America empowered the virtuous... virtue a human characteristic designed to reveal & release the totality of what it means to be human, with humans.

America promised that such a 'CITY ON THE HILL' was possible... BUT ONLY IN THE NATURE OF THE PEOPLE, AS THEY ENGAGED & INTEGRATED WITH EACH OTHER.

ONLY under such social conditions could all the fruits of our labors, the natural resources of our nation, all brought to bear on the needs of all its citizens.

ONY under such conditions CAN EVERY CITIZEN OR VISITOR UNDERSTAND & EXPERIENCE THE AMERICAN EXPERIENCE. BARRING THAT?

FAKE AMERICA... TRUMP'S AMERICA.

THIS IS NOT THE DREAM OF AMERICA... NOR ITS WEALTH.

Black America is not looking for the latest Cadillac for their garage.

They want to wake up, stretch & not have to remember that today, like yesterday, they would have to be on the defensive... the enemy ALWAYS AS CLOSE AS OUR NEIGHBOR.

Today, every day, America promises a land of sacred people, secured by each to the other.

YET TODAY, EVERY DAY, BLACK AMERICA, WOMEN, OTHER COMMUNITIES OF COLOR OR UNIQUE ETHNICITY, WOKE TO FEAR, WENT TO BED WITH FEAR.

TODAY, EVERY DAY, WE HAVE BUT ONE OPPORTUNITY…

TO BE A PATRIOT, STARTS WITH MY NIEGHBOR, EXTENDS TO MY ENEMY.

In word & deed.

Just like Jesus stated.

THE AMERICAN DREAM IS EVERY PARENTS DREAM… this 1st & FOREMOST FOR THEIR CHILDREN… NOT THEMSELVES. A DREAM WHERE THEIR CHILDREN ARE FREE TO BE… HUMAN.

Ask ANY black mother…

America as the 'great' Christian nation: The sinful arrogance of religious nationalism & exceptionalism

("My daddy is 'better' than your daddy...")

"So far, we have had the Constitution backing most of the demands for change, & this has made our work easier, since we could be sure that the federal courts would usually back up our demonstrations legally. Now we are approaching areas where the voice of the Constitution is not very clear. We have left the realm of constituted rights & we are entering the area of human rights." M.L. King, Jr.

"On the day crime dons apparel of innocence–through a curious transposition peculiar to our times–it is innocence that is called upon to justify itself." Albert Camus

"All actions that affect the rights of other men are wrong if their maxim is not consistent with publicity." Immanuel Kant

"Even though Christianity has failed to produce the fruits of true discipleship, the message is still there for the rest of us to acquire, inherit, restore & put to good use... to integrate & to use to reprogram ourselves to a higher order of interpersonal social values." The Last Spiritual Samurai

"The kingdom of God will be taken from you & given to a nation bringing forth the fruits thereof." Jesus

"Fifth Thesis: The greatest problem for the human species, whose solution nature compels it to seek, is to achieve a universal *civil society* administered in accord with the right." Immanuel Kant

Rev. Moon often spoke to members of his church on the providential significance of America. The 1st principle was that God's particular interest in America, even with the natives already there, was the vision of a restored Israel, transplanted into the current times.

Why Israel?

Israel represents a social, cultural, familial standard of socialized citizens, integrated into a national level internal moral identity, one that would serve to inform their emotional identities & behavior, no matter where they might be in the world.

Always Jewish, hence, ALWAYS HUMAN.

The pattern of social development evidenced in Jewish history, fully developed in the treatise, *The ONLY Possible God*, offers that the Jewish people, over a period of 2000 years, were re-educated to a standard of common morality, the likes of which as a means to define a peoples to itself... & to all others, redefines the meaning of evolution.

Given the sociological significance of relationships to humanity, individually or in toto, in the natural form of the development of a social conscience, when it was integrated into the consciousness & authoritatively developed as a cultural evolutionary imperative, offered the Jewish people a socializing experience that perfectly mimics the moral/conscience development every child experiences, in some way & to some degree, in their family life.

The sense of self, of order to the universe, was & is unparalleled as a psychological advantage in a world yet hostile not only to the individual, but also to various forms of communities that formed, along religious, cultural, racially defined & experiential lines.

'Being' Jewish meant one was valued, that one inherently was thus cared for & about & thus, mattered, creating a sense of being' entitled'. Bearing a 'most valued' sense of personal status, even in a hostile world, offered the average person a quality of psychological & therefore, spiritual well-being, authenticity… & social status & authority, ONLY achieved in the healthiest & strongest families & communities.

Thus, in this society of informed & co-created civility, every person shared the same essential value… to themselves, to their neighbor, to their enemy.

A family unit is naturally designed to be fully capable of defending itself, in all the ways meaningful to natural needs. Starting with the socializing of a common identity, that allows & only encourages morally relevant individuality & creativity.

Jews acted as a unified family after the 'visitation' with God, even though established as tribes. The 'principles' to guide all interpersonal relationships, of any kind or duration, were now shared as an 'ordained' value orientation. While it appeared with the authority of an unknown quantity 'God,' the 'faith' of the people was such that this 'power' was to be submitted to. What they could not yet fully fathom, not understanding the ideal of family & the ideal of family values needed to be fully 'human,' was that this God's behavior, when understood from the long view, was the same pattern EVERY parent exercises in the socialization of their children.

Hence, whether it was actually 'God' that was the social agent, the effect of the interpretation of 'God's' various interventions was still of the same sociological significance to humanity, in its potential value, to the Jews… but in the end, as the seeding nation, eventually to all humanity.

The greatest insight to garner from all of this was that however interpreted, as a divine integration & intervention, or a natural form of social evolution, in keeping with human need & potential, Jewish history mimics the natural socialization all families experience & must process, however successfully from a social/moral point of view.

Jesus, in the record of his words, notes how individuals & groups of individuals were NOT honoring the 'law'... themselves. These were those in power who had come to sense that as representing 'God's' interests, should be thus treated equally as if God was there, in their midst, & then to act as the people would treat God, were God there in front of them.

If properly understood & integrated into one's own being, the morality of the '10 words', that God sought humanity cease & desist in the behaviors addressed, & thus, the corresponding motives that were producing the social harms specifically noted, would then create not just a conscientious response, but a developing or maturing the of the desire to care... or love.. Yet, in the multiplication of the '10 words' into hundreds of laws clearly signifies that the people did NOT get the lesson.

The 'idea' is that if I care enough about you, as the source of 'ultra' personal meaning, (imagine parents as gods to the children, in the mind of the child), & you advise me NOT to pull Judy's hair, I will understand it should also naturally imply to not do 'any' other harms to Judy. The social consequence being a co-created justice exists, moving each from the limited sense of self as an individual, into an 'us' identity, thus community is both created & sustained as a morally significant feature for both parties..

Then we co-create & simultaneously experience a natural equality, but based upon an idea that my identity, as a valued & thus socially significant entity, is embedded in my being human, being 'Jewish', but then, this to be with you, too. Hence, acting Jewish, morally as well as in other culturally normative ways.

This required a natural civility in the conducting of oneself with other such 'sacred' entities. A national identity is created, with a moral sense of the cosmos birthed in a 'family' social environment, albeit an artificially created one.

But the idea of using others, as a means to exclusive wealth & privilege, is not a normative feature of such principles. Though Jews held slaves as a 'right', even after the intervention with Moses, Jews were still compelled by the 'law' to not treat others unfairly.

Of course, as now, people do not choose to honor the most emotionally compelling reasons for NOT creating harm, but THEIR conscience is not committed to in the same fashion, with the same weighty cultural reasons for not acting as anarchists on their minds & hearts.

Even with 'God' offering that human harm is a direct result of NOT caring, people did not & do not recognize the social state they create... even to denying their own value, for its unprincipled rebellion that then creates chaos, not ordered chaos, but the kind that harms, when there is cause & means not to so harm.

But as Jesus noted with the scribes & Pharisees, the religious leaders of the time, people should follow their moral prescriptions, being authorities on the law, but he warned NOT to follow their personal public, social & political behaviors, being of the opposite quality demanded to be 'in faith' with God.

Jesus sought to offer a moral contrast to such assumed exceptionalism, arguing such people, when they brought others to God, did no favors, for they burdened the people's hearts in ways no God, nor any parent would approve of. Jesus stated that we each needed to be 'perfect' as our parent in heaven, this evidenced in our capacity to always love, even to our enemy. Yet, do we observe such standards from our pulpits, the inheritors & bearers of Jesus words, & thus, his commission?

Law became a tool of control, not a temporary means of educational confrontation. Had the Jewish people truly used their 'freedom', to honor God, by fully integrating the '10 words' into their hearts, that part of ourselves which is what is sacred to us, that ultimately educates & guides our consciences, in time, the people, as parents & as citizens, would have demonstrated all the characteristics of a natural patriot.

A patriot is the 1ˢᵗ & last defender of a nation's informing values & social & political conscience. Thus, a 'true' Jew, acted with the conscience that honored the 1ˢᵗ parent, God, & thus, would give such a witness in motives & public behaviors that God's words, once articulated to the mind, had not taken root as the core identifying values.

This means, that in all, the 'true' Jew was the ideal human, acting as a child of the God that informed them to not harm one another. This Jew was thus also a patriot, to his/her nation, & thus, a perfect emissary for the 'word of God' to reach other ears, inform other hearts. Of what is possible, what is needed, what aids & humanizes.

The average Jew & their experience then becomes a hope & inspiration for others. Judgment Day arrives. Freedom rings in hearts that had known none. Jewish people then offer what no nation, no people, no family could have imagined.

Inheriting such values, each Jewish child then knew a quality of civility & community only realized in the trenches of such values. But as most cultures & peoples developed various degrees of civility & demanded social morality, the Jewish people were primed for the final push.

That final revelation was in the words of values & the behaviors giving witness, that Jesus sought to offer his own people. As their rightful & God-willed final inheritance.

Today, because of 4 words... simple words, really, but because of these words, Americans were given a form of the original '10 words' offered Moses. And more... so much more.

What made the Jewish people providentially unique & occupying a 'most favored status' was ONLY secured in the faith of a sustained behavior mimicking the words God offered as the guide to the cosmic conscience.

Hence, prophets emerged when the people got too far off track morally.

With Jesus, the final formula for fulfilling the will of God, completing the covenant as to humanity's role, was secured in the renewed effort to not just recognize the will of God, but now to fully commit to it, to include even our enemy in the commitment to community we would hence forth offer as a personal public & political norm.

With Jesus, the will of God was immediate, & immediately available. With the failure to garner the support & co-commitment needed to propagate this deepening of God's will for humanity, to the final effort needed, Jesus, was forced to only offer to the future, what he had to tried to give living witness to.

Instead… we made him God.

America, by including 4 simple words, resurrected the Jesus that the Christians had buried in history. For to honor that 'ALL' are created equal, we have accepted that status for ourselves, as of now a promise that is secured.

BUT ONLY SECURED WITH EACH OTHER.

Equality is a social state of community. If there is no true community, then the evidence of such a personal, public & political state CANNOT be in evidence. Equality is a statement of morally significant reality.

Hence, there is no superiority, assumed or granted. Not economically, socially, politically or religiously. None would thus assert an entitlement, a status, or such moral agency as to justify an greater experience & access to life & its resources.

When clearly understood, either as a providential development of merely one of socially significant social evolution, America, with 4 words, offered us the same freedom 'to be' & to celebrate that fully with others.

As relationships have always suffered the violence of an unbridled, arrogant & self-justifying anarchy that has ruled the world, Jewish history argued that was NOT normal as to what it means 'to be human'. Jesus merely, wisely, offered that the natural conclusion to humanity's most pressing needs & source of harm would ONLY be relieved when we got serious about the quality of care we demanded of ourselves… & thus, offered each other.

Jesus called for maturity in what it means to be human. Maturity in that we accept the reality of our values & then act proactively to address that challenge. Hence, Jews were also thus called to public witness. This orientation then offered in ant environment, to any other person.

Jesus specifically called all humanity to such a standard of care in the story of the 'good' Samaritan. He challenged others to as to who actually acted as a neighbor to the one in need… thus, who then gave the evidence of loving God?

Americans are called to a natural civility.

A civility that then allows EACH & EVERY citizen to have the same quality access to the 'freedoms' that have been denied so many in history… & still are being denied to this day. Freedom of speech was meant to be a shared opportunity… not the domain of the powerful, the anarchist, nor especially the rhetorical terrorist such as we have in POTUS.

To offer an exercise of the freedom of speech that intentionally seeks to harm others?

Actually, unconstitutional.

If my exercise of my freedoms here, inhibit your equal opportunity, in the personal exercise of those behaviors, then we have, with impunity, violated the very purpose for which this country was sought, for which a God would seek to guide, if that God does exist.

God sought, history seeks, a nation of humans acting ONLY as humans must, to be human.

Which translates into a recognized, mature acceptance of the need for & value of morally significant, sustainable relationships, this 'normative' expectation both honors the 1st civil right & social obligation, we also act as the cosmos in its wisdom, to bring about life… & the human body.

Hence, the founders intended a values orientation that in the moral fulfillment of its indicated & needed social expression would bring into existence such a social state of sustainable community that had not so existed since the height of the Jewish state, as an image of God's future hope for all humanity.

Hence, America merely establishes what EVERY person needs, naturally is entitled to, once humanity reasons rationally about the nature of reality & its natural demands we must honor, to justify our existence.

Thus, as a patriot, my family is the 1st recipient of America's promise. I teach this value to my child… She shares it where she goes. She is our budding patriot. Then, my neighbor, next door, or the illegal one seeking refuge here, or the country that needs me there, to offer my body in defense of those values, I thus defend those values even to my friend not more than to my enemy.

My citizenship entitles me to certain social, public & political opportunities. In this, I act mostly as a consumer. Until my path crosses my neighbor, my enemy… then I act as a patriot. Not seeking to diminish others in their same exercise & desires for sanctuary & a mutually shared & sacred environment.

This is even applied as a national guiding policy in my dealing with the world.

Remember… ALL were created equal, by nature or nature's God, we have thus reasoned & offered this as the state of what it means 'to be human'.

Hence, in the end, to be an 'American' has no less obligation & benefit, to being human, that 'to be Jewish', as a true Jew would envision it, them & their neighbor, & their God…

America demands no less….

TO BE AN AMERICAN, TO BE HUMAN, ONE MUST HONOR THE 1ST CIVIL RIGHT…

Behavior bestows true status. ONLY offered to others, as the measure of our psychological & social health, to measure our commitment to what it demands to truly be an American, a patriot.

The will to care enough to create "ALL… are created" wherever we go, with whomever we encounter, even our enemy.

IF YOU CAN'T OR WON'T DO THAT?

YOU ARE NOT CHRISTIAN, A PATRIOT & MERELY AN AMERICAN BECAUSE OF SOCIAL ACCEPTANCE OF BIRTH OR OTHER FACTORS, NOT BECAUSE ONE CHOOSES TO 'BE JEWISH/AMERICAN/HUMAN.

The 3 Great Heresies of Americans: Evil is NOT a protected right

"He ain't heavy... he's my brother..."

"The Constitution protects my right to hate whoever I want..." A Trump devotee

"I refuse to accept the idea that the 'isness' of man's present nature makes him morally incapable of reaching up for the eternal 'oughtness' that forever confronts him." M.L. King, Jr.

"(the rebel's)... only virtue will lie in never yielding to the impulse to allow himself to be engulfed in the shadows that surround him & in obstinately dragging the chains of evil, with which he is bound, toward the light of good." Albert Camus

"The world cannot hate you; but me it hateth, because I testify of it, that the works thereof are evil." Jesus

There can be no true pleasure in harming another human being. That is not to say there is no emotionally significant association with harming others, merely that it is not true pleasure.

When a Trump cult member asserted that the Bill of Rights protected not only his spoken words, but that it also protected the content, he couldn't have been more wrong.

To assert that ANYTHING in the Constitution or Bill of Rights legitimates the quality of anti-social values that would not only justify racism, but advance it as a moral option under the auspices of the Constitution, is either arrogance beyond the pale, madness or immaturity.

Actually, it is all three.

There are many examples of those who sought to rebel against the 'status quo'. But of one moral grouping, these were the universalists, the righteous defenders of the unique & precious innate & absolute natural value of each person, these are the righteous rebels of history.

Such righteous rebels argued that history was to serve humanity, not be tortured by it. The key always lying within the grasp of all... the choice in how much we will commit to caring, beyond self-serving interest.

There is one word that is most often offered with blood, sweat & tears, silently whispered & held sacred in the hearts of the powerless... the simple word: justice.

Justice is in all actuality a mathematical statement of equation. It is the sum of the hearts of integration, offered in an effort to realize community as a civil & cultural state. The equation when fully fleshed out? Beloved community.

The Amendment process in America serves two psychological functions. By its very existence, as a promoted & sacred process, it offers that the community & its individuals are to be recognized as so sacred, that as the social conscience & thus commitment to community advances in its moral considerations 'evolve' such that the present & past are not the true measure of care needed & justified, then humanity can both accept the judgement & thus support such public evolutions... & that in acting to realize such values in the behavior of the people, we effectively participate in a natural form of repentance, hence, in the growth of character, celebrate the very nature of life, as it progressed.

The end of slavery was not truly the Day of Judgement, for it as an institution, nor also as the evil value it was. For the heart of arrogance, the sense of a divine entitlement, was sustained & NEVER repented.

For under the cover of 'culture', the bias, the hate, the commitment to harm & depravation was… & IS SUSTAINED AS A RIGHT TO THIS DAY.

On two plains of reasoning this is not only wrong, but evil.

Racism, sexism, environmental enslavement, all speak to the exclusivity of right to manipulate others, for 'profit'. The profit being any advantage, benefit, personal, public or political, that offers an entitlement not unilaterally shared, that has a moral significance of disadvantage to some party.

Given that the 1st Principle of Americanism is to honor that ALL are created equal, then this immediately argues against ANY kind or quality of exploitation, diminishment or other form of debilitating discrimination. No matter how framed as some extension of civil rights defended by the Bill of Rights, the 'supreme' value implicitly argues for a social or cultural justice to be the norm.

If we honor that 1st civil principle, then in terms of what it means to love another, we are well on our way to becoming a patriot… the defender of the values of the realm.

Yet, ever since the 1st Americans had to decide on God or mammon, the choice was made… & never repented. Some sought the rhetorical means to persuade & flatter until one imagines even God willed what is, of else why are we so successful at it?

It is not natural to hate… it is learned.

Want to understand the psychological burden it creates? Take an infant…only express hate in every form available… as a sustained diet, for weeks, months, years; then seek its humanity. If your imagination fails you…

Religious communities hold that sin is both that done against oneself as well as what is done to others or the environment. It speaks to willed & substantially created harm… an atheism of commitment to care.

Moses was instructed to inform the people that they kinds of harms they had allowed & entertained previously could stand no longer… GOD WAS AMENDING THE NATURE OF THE RELATIONSHIP.

If this is a 'Christian' country, then one must ask… when did Jesus offer that the Jewish laws did NOT somehow apply any longer or did not apply to Christians? Love God… love your neighbor as oneself.

There is thus a dual demand for a standard of civil human that would be no less than Jew was to Jew. Honor in the social reality our fealty to the 1st Principle of all being created equal, with its inherent moral expectation; this to be a patriot/citizen. 2nd, to love our neighbor as ourselves, as good Jews ourselves, in the honoring of Jesus, but then, like Jesus demanded of his own people at that time… to be a true child of God, our commitment to our neighbor is also even to our enemy. Hence, as patriots, we still defend our neighbor in that civil & political significance we must hold to & for each other.

When we so 'hate' one another, it is our sister we hate, it is our brother we have chosen to hate… it is family. It is our wife, our husband, our parent, our child. For as we have chosen to honor the least, it is also then the judgement on the whole. For if one is diminished, in the context of the whole, of the 'all', none now have love, none now have community, none now have sanctuary. For in America, as in being Jewish, my identity, my security, my value, my very being is ONLY secured in my neighbor. He bears witness to the world to that which I cannot… his commitment to America.

When I love… I create co-community. When I co-create community, we are the resulting justice. Our integration, the summation of heart, the result of freedom used as only it can be, to care for others.

If we do not love, we deny our own need for community & the psychological benefits that naturally occur. Love is merely a quality of commitment, substantialized over time as a 'way of being' in the intersection with the need for interpersonal relationships & intercourse. Hence, love is a rational act, chosen for its value to the purposes chosen… community.

In both the stated moral civic orientation demanded by the 1st Principle of America, & in the natural need for & benefit of community, to act against such compelling rationales for social action, then we act as a deviant. Deviant in the harms created, both external in the political reality between people, but also in the internal states that are potentially created as sustained psychological states.

Racism, sexism & an entitlement of unprincipled use of the creation is irrational as a moral consideration, as a social state of relationship, as a human response to the nature of the very cosmos itself. Hence, it reveals our irrationality. It forces irrationality on its victims. Who can truly process such sustained irrationality, offered as living fare, all one's life?

Only Jesus, & Jewish history offer us respite.

In the meantime, racism, sexism, environmental exploitation, are all irrational values, in the context of human nature, need & the nature of life itself.

Those self-serving values are the essence of anti-social, unscientific, emotionally self-centered atheism. Experienced by others, they express an unearned & unjustified arrogance, entitlement & an imagined exceptionalism. It forces 'profit' to ALWAYS BE GOD. Hence, unknown to such people, THE RACIST, THE SEXIST, THE ENVIROMENTAL EXPLOITER, ARE ALL ATHEISTS. Behavior in the noon day sun always reveals what even evil wanted to brag about… "I may be evil… but I exist!"

Such people place themselves even above any God in popular imagination. Hence, they cannot truly honor ANY god, except themselves. Since it is they who have assumed the moral authority to usurp the words of Jesus & the words of common sense that American enshrined… honor all others as equal to oneself & then act accordingly.

The social impact of morally entertained madness?

Rape, slavery, child abuse, parental abuse, spousal abuse, environmental exploitation & abuse, economic deprivation, divorce, pedophilia, murder, torture, slavery of children & women, slavery of ethnic & religious minorities, terrorism, deprogramming & religious kidnapping.

"I can hate whom I will hate because the Constitution protects my freedom of belief…"

All because someone imagines that to be human, to be an American…means that they can be evil.

Such people live here in America… but they are NEVER patriots… they exist as the lowest form of citizen.
The self-entitled capitalist consumer.

Black & Baptized by the Blues: 'Sin eaters' digesting the 'evil' of human experience

It is the time to declare a National Day of Shame & Repentance for the Institution of American Slavery

"The Constitution protects my right to hate whoever I want." American white Christian nationalist

There are probably few less true & more ignorant statements that I have had to suffer hearing in America, than the one above.

He is critically wrong on several fronts.

#1. America nor her Constitution protects such rhetoric, as idea or as communication.

#2. Such racist notions are actually denied by America as a civil right because it violates the very 1st civil right offered all under the umbrella of her legal commitments.

#3. As such, his posture is not only unpatriotic, it is un-American to its rotted ideological core.

4. Behaviorally acted upon, it is close to treason. It seeks to usurp the norms of morality insisted upon so that the nation's purpose, to establish a state of such sacred individuals as sacred & equal individual private, social & political entities, that the normal abuses suffered at the hands of others, acting as governments, entitled & entrenched, would now be forever set aside for a share in a co-created sanctuary.

There is no more distinguishing mark of shame & immorality on a nation than that based on the incivility &

immaturity of morality of white America, not only for the racism that produced slavery, but the arrogance & outright evil misuse of Christianity & Jesus that is perpetrated here on these shores. That is sustained to this very day.

The degradation of our nation, Jesus & the American people was effected for the least defensible reason.

"WE CHOOSE TO BE RACISTS... BE DAMNED OUR GOD, BE DAMNED OUR JESUS, BE DAMNED OUR NATION. OUR WILL, OUR EMOTIONALLY INFORMED VALUES, NOT THOSE OF GOD, OR MAN, MATTERS.

ONLY WE MATTER."

ML King once remarked on the fact that black America had to make a choice... by what values would such Americans come to define themselves, as humans, suffering over millennia the psychological assault of an ideological form of hate & thus, interpersonal, public & political terrorism. Would they be so tempted by the hate they must digest EVERY day, from birth to death, to act as Cain did, when his brother became arrogant that 'God' had accepted HIS offering, but not his brother Cain's?

Would those 'forced' to be 'Cain's, by white people, not God, would they allow the hate of a brother (from the wannabe 'Abel') tempt one to return hate for hate... even to expand it to the physical plane? Would those forced to the humiliation that another offers as our 'just dues" then seek the blood of those who set us in hell? Can such arrogant people not then expect us not to rebel?

Is not EVERY black American entitled to justice TODAY? A justice that acknowledges that what happened in the past, was evil, is evil. Has yet to be confronted in the noon day sun, for its evil, for its inhumanity, for its violation of EVERYTHING that is truly America & American. Is it not PAST TIME FOR AN ACCOUNTING, A PUBLIC ACCOUNTING... NOT OF HUMILIATION, BUT OF THE CLEANSING EXPERIENCE OF SHAME, A HEALTHY SHAME THAT MOVES US TO BE PROACTIVE IN RESTORATIONAL PATTERNS OF REPENTANCE?

Is it not time, to offer, 'yes, we were wrong... WE ARE WRONG & we deeply harm & alienate part of the American family? For this, we deeply repent as a nation."

King sought justice for black Americans, in the securing of the rights that were theirs, but had been denied in every way imaginable, unethical & illegal. King sought that people not react violently, to move history, but offer the community affirming values of non-violent protest. Hence, he asked them to 'keep' caring but in ways to sustain the potential for community, always revealing the potential for creating the ideal, beloved community. By persuading others that the times demanded a greater measure of what it meant & means 'to be human', being human. King noted that violence was an option. King noted that MAYBE forgiveness was the ONLY way to save & salvage Americans, much less the nation.

I will argue even further than King. I will argue that since the 1st slave found themselves here, that black America has been the righteous 'sin eaters' ever since. That THIS digesting of hate, this digesting of the sins of the white man, liberated black America NOT TO BE TEMPTED TO REBEL AS REVOLUTION... SEEKING THE DEMISE OF THE ENEMY, RATHER THAN HIS RESTORATION.

I will assert even further that even with the Christianity that was forced upon them, where the ultimate message of Jesus is the need to love our enemy, forgiving as we were forgiven by God, it was NOT Christianity that provided & provides what black America needed, & needs to not only survive, but prosper in spite of such experiences. No, black America came here with the human values needed to survive such hate... black America provided for itself. Her mama's knew the secret to life... even hard life.

One must have the heart of a parent, to suffer all that our children may offer, may thrust at the world, in hate, confusion, immaturity. Africa may seem materially challenged. But America today proves that the wealth of a nation is not measured in its economic & political ability to manipulate & controls others for personal gain.

Rather, EVEN IN THIS world, gratitude for life, is actually & ONLY realized in the unconditional offerings we place before one another, as the measure of OUR OWN WORTH.

Hence, to NOT KILL...in response to hate & intentional harm... is a blessing. Of heart... led by the evolutionarily inspired. Inspired by the rationale to not seek equal harm, is to choose to use one's most precious opportunity... our will to be. Mother's understand this principle. It is why we call them mothers… not for the breast milk that nourished us to this day of reckoning. Mothers teach, in their sustained behaviors, what it means to be committed to the welfare of others, even to offering one's own life.

By NOT killing.

Today, to the world, white America is bankrupt morally, without heart or principle. Because of this, in terms of recognizable behavior, America is no longer, if it ever was… human. Thus, not fit to lead. Needing a doctor.

Black America may be the doctor ordered.

The reason not to return hate for hate, harm for harm, comes from our deeper sense of our humanity, that argues not to escalate, but seek to temper, to manage towards a mutuality of benefit… & hence respect & care.

When we are assaulted by the hate of others, even if imagined as some 'justice/revenge' for the past, the person so subjected to such treatment must find some means to digest, or otherwise process such hate.

Naturally, when we are 1st confronted with the evil that men do, we are almost shocked into submission. Only in time do we begin to entertain the medley of emotional & rational options that might occur to us, from our own experiences or from the wisdom of others. 1st we suffer shock, then disappointment & despair. Why is this happening? Then, as we seek response, we also seek means to confront & require a 'cease & desist' in the experience… & an accounting of 'why'.

Naturally, those so inclined have an equally diverse medley of responses that only further act to negate our shared human value. We then experience a resentment. The assessment that what has transpired MUST cease & we begin to act in that defense. If we encounter an overwhelming force of response to such confrontation, we may discover we are completely out of any proactive confrontational models, means & opportunities.

How to not hate in kind?

1st order of wisdom?

Survive.

2nd order of business. Understand 'who' you are. What did your mama teach you? To hold a vision of self that survives all that life forces us to bear… our burden or for other's. Never to relinquish this identity of sacredness. Even onto the last breath under the whip… "I loved life as I could… to it I now surrender, in my last offering of gratitude. TO NOT CURSE THE ENEMY THAT NOW BRINGS ME TO MY KNEES... UNREPENTANT FOR BEING... HUMAN." Even as that being sinks beyond the pale of what it MUST mean, 'to be human'.

In that failure to curse... black America forgave, forgives, offers, even to this day... offering yet a hand up. But a hand that 1st must be embraced.

For centuries now, black America has digested the sins of America, the sins of white Americans, the sins of those who claim to be 'Christian'. In not rebelling, in not seeking revenge... black America loved its enemy. What more can ANY people offer, to prove their true humanity... WORTHY TO BE LOVED & WORTHY TO BE LOVED BY...

The institutional refusal to deny racism & its bastard child, slavery, is the continual witness to that truth that NO CHRISTIAN NATION OCCUPIES THE SHORES FROM CALIFORNIA TO MAINE.

How much longer must black America stand alone, bear alone the weight of the hope of a nation, forced to be offered on bended knee?

How long must they forgive an enemy that NEVER matures?

Be advised to let no racism, religious intolerance, political ideology or personal experience to tempt you to scorn God's Way- your parent knows your suffering & suffers more...

Remember, you were 1st of all God's children & must yet return to that status. Do not suffer to learn the art of self-deception. It is an even greater enemy to you than the slave owner who keeps you in psychological & physical bondage. Instead, learn the sad lesson the child denied & abused must suffer when they, too, rebel, but to reject. For them, too, all seems lost & without morally significant comfort or options.

Then, we are most tempted & most certain to kill our brother, as Cain came to kill Abel.

For if we allow our past to dictate the path of the present, to choose to call for the blood of those who have oppressed us, we will discover too late, that the blood of a brother, cast upon the sands of time, cannot be erased. But only remembered.

"All... are" vs the Bill of Rights: Power politics as the practice of immorality

"We will reach the goal of freedom... all over the nation, because the goal of America is freedom. Abused & scorned though we may be, our destiny is tied up with the destiny of America." M.L. King, Jr

"But communists, fascists, terrorists of all ilk, domestic & foreign, Nazi's & American racist white nationalists, all worship the same god... choose who & what you hate, then proceed to destroy what you hate, by any means possible. Hence, never admitting that while the opposite side is the enemy, as communist encounters white nationalist, they agree on one thing... the tools to persuade, that begin with hateful rhetoric & end with bullets." The Last Spiritual Samurai

"What is needed is a realization that power without love is reckless & abusive, & love without power is sentimental & anemic. Power at its best is love implementing the demands of justice, & justice at its best is power correcting everything that stands against love. And this is what we must see as we move on... It is precisely this collision of immoral power & powerless morality which constitutes the major crisis of our times." M.L. King, Jr

"... I provisionally defined morality as a science that teaches, not how we can be happy, but how we ought to become worthy of happiness." Immanuel Kant

"The problem of establishing a perfect civil constitution depends upon the problem of law governed <u>external relations among nations (or people)</u> & cannot be solved until the latter is." Immanuel Kant

Today I heard a right wing propagandist offer that lies should be afforded the same social significance & protection as truth… all protected as a matter of 'free speech.'

One of the greatest errors of both understanding & judging the personal & social significance of the Constitution & the Bill of Rights is to assume that America & her founding documents are all about the rights of humanity.

This false notion of the sanctity of ANYTHING declared a 'right' then assumes the moral authority of the nation, is the arrogance that Jesus assured led straight to hell.

That is the greatest failure, that will lead to all other such failures; our assuming some moral 'right' to both embrace racism & then, subsequently, to give it such morally significant social expression as we create a social climate of inequality. This behavioral & rhetorical communication was & is still fully intended, so that black America is left in no doubt as to its meaning. Offered, mind you, like some kind of reverse vitamin, that rather than enhancing life, is intended to deprive & debilitate, emotionally & psychologically.

AMERICA IS NOT MERELY NOR JUST A NATION DEDICATED TO THE PROTECTION OF INDIVIDUAL RIGHTS as its prime directive… rather, AMERICA IS A NATION DEFINED BY SUCH VALUES

THAT THE INTEGRITY & ULTIMATE SACRED VALUE OF THE INDIVIDUAL IS NOT ONLY ARTICULATED AS SUCH, BUT DEFENDED & CARRIED FORTH AS THE TOTALITY OF ITS NATIONAL MISSION & COVENANT.

AMERICA IS A NATION DEFINED BY HER VALUES, DEFENDING THE SACRED VALUE OF THE INDIVIDUAL, HENCE... ALL PEOPLE. UNIVERSALLY.

There is no more important understanding about the potential greatness of American than to fully digest the significance of such a mission, what it means to the average citizen, & what it offers the world. For what can be imagined & created by one, can be duplicated by another, with the same knowledge, the same values informing our activities.

Most Americans assume, a most egregious & especially challenging error at this time in history, is the self-serving interpretation that America is just about freedom & rights.

Those are merely words to describe a more central & founding awareness.

It is in the demand for an equality of a shared social recognition of the innate value each person naturally develops, as a cognitive awareness of the significance of their own life, that demands then a qualifying social environment that can sustain such value, in the encounter with others. This thus demanding such a quality of civil behavior that community can thus be not only achieved as a matter of social contract, but comes to be the core 'heart' of citizenship, this then producing the natural patriot.

That natural patriot merely the social expression, in civil terms, of such willingness to social & political integration with others, that beloved community is its natural fruit.

This dynamic, of a nation conceived on the founding principle of equality, then demands the natural discipline every psychologically healthy family will teach, by example & by cognitive education.

If we are to be an honorable people, honorable as individuals, then the priority is the civility that insures all the community in the same quality of experience, with each other, as with any.

There are those who imagine that some 'belief' about life, religious in most cases, allows them a sense of such morality that the rest of us do not share, that they, in their moral superiority, thus have some 'greater' civil right & responsibility. This self-defined & self-authorized power & authority, to dominate others, even in their experience of & expression of those same civil rights to be shared, is allowed to be absolute.

This absoluteness, created in the passage & expression of laws, is designed specifically to undermine, limit or inhibit others use of such civil rights. The same civil rights now brought AGAINST the individual, social & political interests of others.

The greatest examples being slavery & abortion.

In BOTH cases, a more powerful group brought personally held religious belief as the defining authority for political exceptionalism, that was used to morally justify limiting the same freedoms that others demand, even in such politically motivated behavior.

If one is arrogant enough to declare this a 'Christian' nation, then the totality of Jesus' values then are demanded, as a social norm, not just as a band aid for moral domination & subjugation of others.

Unfortunately, the moral education & the degree of genuine intelligence sought by the average white person, as a living statement of the moral significance they both commit to & seek to integrate with today, has little to do with establishing within oneself a pillar of such values as to naturally define a patriot.

There is NO national leadership truly speaking to the values America demands when she defends, every day, those same 4 words, to the same & the emerging audiences that need to consider them... BEFORE THEY ACT WITH ONE ANOTHER.

THE 1ST TIER SOCIAL VALUE OF AMERICA IS THE DEMAND TO HONOR ONESELF, BY HONORING

ALL OTHERS, AS EQUAL, IN ALL THE WAYS THAT DEFINE WHAT IT MEANS TO BE HUMAN, BECOMING HUMAN. This to define the essential American, being an American.

The 2nd tier of values defended in America, are the behaviors that ANY human would seek to embrace as their own, as the means to integration into & to co-create, beloved community… of the 'just' society. We know this 2nd tier of defended & articulated values as the Bill of Rights, with her evolving social conscience, known as Amendments.

We 'amend' that which is not complete, clear… & moral. Here is revealed the wisdom & heart of the founders towards the future.

Slavery was considered a 'God' given right, thus, not to be tampered with by man. We know now the 1st con that was perpetrated was to fool the man in the mirror long enough to offer such an idea with a straight face. THAT deception accomplished, then the man next door, if he has proceeded on the same assumption, will offer such common signal that both are comforted by the knowledge they share the same secret.

The 1st lie that must be sold… to the self.

Then, if we affirm to each other that we share that commitment, then community is created… & power now to enforce slavery possible. We can imagine "we are doing them niggers a favor, giving their miserable lives meaning…"

Slavery, like sexism, like environmental exploitation & unprincipled domination, all these behaviors are NOT defended, articulated or given any 'freedom' of existence or right to impose on others, as normative behaviors & social experience.

To wrap the issue of abortion on some manipulated science, to control others civil behaviors, is the arrogance neither Jesus NOR God EVER exercises over such people. By what authority do they then act over others?

Further, for Christians, the ONLY people with ANY reason to assert such moral authority, assuming that THEY, & THEY ALONE KNOW & SPEAK FOR GOD, given the evidence of its own history, is the most immoral act of all.

Further, the failure to monitor & control the sexual behavior of those with power over women & children, then to deny it & not take it fully to task? The divorce rate greater than the nation, where is the moral authority to speak to the sexual morals of anyone else?

Then, Christians, the ones MOST fighting universal health care, that don't care for all the babies not wanted, that then suffer for such want, then become our new deviants, alcoholics, drug addicts, criminals & deviant & evil bosses, parents & politicians.

Christians decry food stamps, welfare, but want to force more women, to have children they don't want, such children then forced to suffer for EVERYONE'S LACK OF COMMITMENT TO CARE FOR THEM, ONCE BORN.

Systemic racism, like its sibling, systemic sexism, are the fruit of the values of people... lived. Jesus made it very clear about such people. Majority or not... create a racist & sexist state if you will... but you will suffer for it eternally.

SO, CELEBRATE YOUR POWER TO HARM & LIMIT OTHERS CELEBRATION OF THE VERY FREEDOMS YOU USED TO HARM WITH. BUT DO NOT EXPECT GOD OR JESUS TO BE GREETING YOU AT THE PEARLY GATES.

Jesus made it VERY clear.

BUT NO ELDERS ARE WARNING YOU.

If you will be judged FOR EVERY WORD UTTERED, IF EVERY WORD UTTERED IS ENOUGH TO ENSURE ETERNAL DAMNATION, JUST WHAT DO YOU THINK THE SENTENCE SHOULD BE FOR BEING A RACIST & SEXIST WHO VIOLATED THE VALUES OF AMERICA, A NATION CREATED TO GIVE TRUE HOPE TO THE WORLD... AS TO WHAT IT REALLY MEANS TO BE HUMAN, BEING HUMAN?

I doubt Trump will be around to defend you...

Managing the 'God-seed': Emotional identity as the privatization of the moral self& social conscience

(I keep for me alone, & thus...)

"...be ye therefore perfect, as your father-parent in heaven..." Jesus

"... the human race's irresistible urge to depart from the path marked by nature toward developing its capacities for goodness... thus man made himself unworthy of existing as a species to rule over the earth..." Immanuel Kant

"There is a cosmic difference between heart... & emotion. One is the capacity to care, the other a physiological response to stimuli, natural or artificial, physical in origin or interpreted meanings derived from experience. They can be integrated to create a complete experience of the timeless with the moment." The Last Spiritual Samurai

"Be ye therefore perfect as your father in heaven." Jesus

"In what sense then is there a human nature, a specific nature that is common to all the species? The answer can be given in a single word: *potentialities*. Human nature that is constituted by all the potentialities that are the species-specific properties common to all the human species. Man is to a great extent a self-made creature. Given a range of potentialities at birth, he makes of himself what he becomes by how freely he chooses to develop those potentialities by the habits he forms." Mortimer J Adler

"I had hoped that the white moderates would understand that law & order exist for the purpose of establishing justice, & that when they fail to do this, they become dangerously structured dams that block the flow of social progress." M.L. King, Jr.

"Primary among the resources available to the human quest are, of course, those features of its own nature that best equip it to respond to the obstacles met in living. The continued advancement of these characteristics constitutes the evolutionary development of *homo sapiens*. If we can identify these features, we will have located the evolutionary ground of moral value; for such attributes are valuable precisely because they are essential to the continuance & extension of humanity. An individual cannot aim his/her conduct at the survival of the species, but one can aim at nurturing those natural capacities upon which species-survival depends.

In the human being, cultivation of survival attributes has become a conscious end. We can find human endeavor conduct that aims not merely at securing & maintaining personal well-being & continuance, but also enhancing our native potencies. We are unique among life-forms on this planet in being able to affect deliberately our own continued evolution – not our physical but... our cultural evolution."
Christopher Lyle Johnston

The 'god-seed'... the capacity to care... & the physical body with the rational capacity to act & 'choose' how & why we are caring'...

Humanity is at an impasse with itself. Relationships continue to emerge as the universal, & eternal Achille's Heel, the point of no return, the ultimate & final enemy. This unmet challenge haunts us throughout human history. Our greatest desires seem thwarted at every juncture for opportunity for change.

Today, in the notions of freedom that are emerging as social norms, we observe & experience such a privatization of the moral self, that there is a dwindling effect of any evidence of a social conscience either as a social value or as a personal statement of integrity & attendance to the values of our nation. Values that demand we honor one another as equal to the opportunity & freedoms defined & defended as a nationally protected inheritance. There is neither national conscience nor any social conscience. Christianity is merely a whisper of authority for any social or political standard of commitment 'to care.'

The one universal constant in human experience, that bridges all times, all peoples, all religions, is that all humanity knows suffering & we know it from birth… not all experience love, either as its source, or as its recipient. This suffering observed & experienced is merely the fruit of the values that have informed our intercourse with one another. Hence, in every sense of the word & in every social environment available to us, our commitment to the principles of civility have perfectly reflected the values we have chosen, consciously or unconsciously. These assumptions have led to habits, then defining a 'human nature' that is a poor example of a morally significant & worthy human 'instinct'.

The challenge, as it always was, is awaiting humanity.

By what definition shall I imagine myself, as the foundation from which do define you, to me.

This is the significance of family.

This is the challenge offered to us by history, as our 'natural' inheritance, the fruit of the architecture of the values we were exposed to, hence experienced, plus what other options were or are provided by our environments, such as church, extended family & friends, even enemies.

The need for moral consideration of our value orientation emerges in both the natural need for interpersonal relationships, but also in the fact that they provide the stimulus' needed to provide for the depth of meaning humanity seeks both in experience & in the quality of the interpersonal relationships that are available or can be accessed.

In the general & specific need for relationships, civility, the commitment to a covenant of sociality in both physical space & proximity, but also in terms of the moral significance of the sought-after social intercourse, is elevated to a tier one level of consideration. Thus, civility emerges as the measure of the commitment we offer, as the living value assigned to the 'other' & our commitment to honor that value in behavior. In the reasoned recognition of the 'need' & unavoidability of relationships to human life & living, we come to grudgingly accept the reality of the value of moving beyond mere & only self-interest.

Religions, in the search for ultimate reality & the forces, processes & principles that instruct & form the nature of the physical cosmos, also encountered not only the need for a sustainable civility, they also discovered that their 'gods' made moral demands upon them. The moral nature of the demands offered significance in two directions… vertical, as in sources of power or social authority & horizontal, as in the relationships more informal & involving varying degrees of power & authority affecting the relationships.

Moral demands made from above emerged in two contexts… natural authority & the authority of 'force'. Natural authority is a contextual authority. Parents, teachers, leaders of any sort, social, religious, political, all serve in the capacity of an expecting honoring of such authority as the standing social moral norm.

As the '1st' human science, religions served to define the nature of reality, but also sought to understand the 'placement' of humanity in that cosmic reality, as a morally significant actor, at least to itself. This 'search' for reality is in all actuality to serve dual purposes. First, it serves to orient humanity to the nature of the cosmos & thus, helps define limits, opportunities & potentials. Second to this, is the search for the means to morally justify demanding a quality of interpersonal social reality so that human suffering is not the constantly emerging universally sustained reality.

In aid to such concerns, philosophy emerged.

But both, or either, to be an asset to the human experience, should not contribute to the mystery of the world... yet, that is exactly what they do. Where Jesus started with one simple concern, one simple message, one simple value orientation to challenge & forever change the nature of human relationships, religious people instead produced over 500 different encapsulations of THEIR perception of Jesus.

To this day, there is not one unified understanding of Jesus, his words, mission & value to the human unmet challenges or to what it must mean 'to be human'.

This forced the idea of ideologies or systems of values, these to force human history along certain morally significant lines, emerging to capture humanity unprepared. These ideological imperatives allowed their actors as much 'freedom' to harm others as they 'felt' would serve their purposes.

Hundreds of millions have died.

The slaughter continues.

In this vacuum of moral credibility as a morally justified species to exist, in the perfection of its own instincts, the rebel of history is left not only to define & defend a human nature, but it needs to be of such reasonability as to also be so rationally accessible as to be available to all, beyond the challenge of the Tower of Babel that exists in the hearts of humanity.

Such an effort, in the vacuum of general human effort, now considered a Herculean task, then would mark such 'citizens' as 'experts', were such rebels to emerge successful in their quest to confront history so as to expose the factual, systemic & structural inequality of life experiences most humanity suffer daily.

In contrast to the theoretical justifications for a social equality to be asserted as the true human norm, our rhetorical behavior belies this effort & forces it into retreat as every moment for interpersonal intercourse that emerges as human opportunity, we revert to 'what we feel' is most important, at least in that emerging time frame.

In lieu of the effort needed for the natural moral human to emerge as a sustainable social creature, governments are needed, to act as the 2nd tier defense of the family & its social & socializing value as a social phenomenon, with various social roles/opportunities uniquely available to those acting as parent/socializing agents.

Into this emerging social need for a sustainable agency for preventing & discouraging the deviance that creates individual & social harm, reason & rationality rise to the surface of needed assets & skill. Now, where emotional 'reasoning' was the source values for interpersonal integration, what could be reasoned but was not reasonable, could now be equally confronted rationally, with moral reasoning offering a new paradigm for defining the nature of acceptable forms of civility, this creating in turn, community.

With reasoning now offered as a 'profitable' skill set, humanity set the stage to demand that 'justice' exists between social actors. Justice merely the demand that the 'norm' for social intercourse MUST NATURALLY also serve to prevent harm, as a sanctioned or allowable opportunity. Hence, humanity sought to prescribe & circumvent previous freedoms, those taken not to aid any except those with the power to ONLY serve self-interest.

Justice emerges in the imagination of a relationship of such equitable boundaries that no harm can emerge, as the result of a moral languishment in the motives affecting the care exercised towards others.

Justice, to exist, argues a state of morally significant & satisfying intercourse is the sustained social state. A 'we' then exists in such a state in time & space that 'we' can declare that community exists, but not simply community... but 'beloved' community. Justice is a social state in which such equitability exists that defenses are not needed; full integration of the individual, as a caring entity, is thus authenticated as the desired norm, that there is neither motive to harm nor is there such a lack of care that harm can merely emerge as a state of neglect.

Justice argues not just proximity to one another, but a full integration of heart, the capacity to care that we rationally act upon, this expressed in our social conscience. This morally significant commitment to & behavioral expression of 'care' is simply the act to integrate, as a living meaning to the behavior. We 'love' the other, the degree of commitment to civility the measure of our 'love' or its absence.

In this social scenario, equitable relationship is merely the outcome of human interaction that honors the personal, public, political & cosmic significance of healthy relationship to life & living. It is the 'maturity' of a species who recognizes both the nature of life but also the implied wisdom offered in its own witness of 'being'. Life exists because such morally significant & sustainable relationships have come to exist that complexity, specialization & even sentience could emerge as equally sustainable states.

Justice for humanity is merely life in a state of such moral equilibrium & stasis that a specific ecological environment is created, as a co-created participatory existence. Into this 'creation' is also created a 4th dimension, that of a sustained, cooperatively assigned meaning & significance. Justice thus serves as a statement of relationship, into which all parties share in creation & the fruits of such effort. Justice then exists in all directions, those in vertical or horizontal qualities or states of relationship.

In contrast to this, is the existence of the tension created when there is no such moral integration of either purpose or meaning. It is obvious, that what can be imagined & willed into existence as the expression of sought meanings as integration provides & effort justifies, rationality & reasoning are equally to be the agents of change to create harm, in the moment or as a sustained social state.

We hate, because we choose to hate.

Even if we were taught to hate, by experience & by education, we still MUST make a choice. Yet, also ONLY in choosing, by refusing to hate & harm, can we be free to seek for a correlative wisdom that our bodies themselves argue MUST be a better alternative. In such acts, then one defends not self nor other… rather, the freedom just to be, our 'isness' as a life form. Only in such retrospect can we fully appreciate the death that is created in every action based upon anti-social values. ONLY then can we fully know the wisdom of freedom thus employed, for the 'goodness' & community it releases as not just a potential, but as a viable, independent form of life.

It is in such uses of freedom, to choose to enter into such a covenant, that the full uniqueness of each individual is released to its full creativity. Paradoxically, it is ONLY in relationship that ANY individual can realize their full human potential. We are always a part of a greater environment, never the sole environmental reality. Not only that, but it is with the resources the environment provides, creatively employed, that we also secure the quality of meaning that also forms the basis for human happiness… which also occurs as a result of a quality of potential ONLY realized in morally sustainable relationships.

Cain kills Abel: Emotional identity as 'god'

Yet, it is also in the quality of the moral motives we entertain that determine what is deviance. Deviance needing to be assigned to such behaviors as either reveal uncivil motives or harmful environmental impact, on people or the natural environment. Deviance emerging in the anti-social values that inhibit & prevent the emergence of true integration into community.

But this is the effect of the choices we make, well informed or not, morally accountable or not. Yet, WHY do we make SUCH DECISIONS? IS IT MERELY A RATIONAL PROCESS? HAVE WE REALLY EVALUATED THE MORAL SIGNIFICANCE OF EVERY IMPULSE THAT WE ACT UPON? IF NOT, WHAT QUALITY OF STIMULUS DO WE GIVE CARTE BLANCHE TO?

This question leads us to the heart of the challenge… the 'authority' we presume to allow our emotional identity.

We each develop our emotional identity in the last trimester as a fetus. During this time, our memories are also working as a physical system. The rational part of the brain though, does not start functioning until after birth, & continues to mature well into the 20's for men.

Social scientists now acknowledge much psychological harm is experienced by every fetus, in the social, psychological & living experiences of expectant mothers & the resultant effect upon mother, her body & hence, the fetus. The impacts, as isolated events or as patterns as emotionally recognizable & encased in emotionally only held memories. The rational part of the brain not engaged until birth.

Hence, the ONLY RATIONALITY AVAILABLE TO THE BABY UPON BIRTH IS THAT WHICH WAS CREATED IN THE LAST TRIMESTER, WHICH IS 100% EMOTIONALLY BASED, THOUGH THERE IS NO MEANS TO COGNITIVELY BRING BACK SUCH MEMORIES, IN THAT THE RATIONAL PART OF THE BRAIN, NEEDED FOR SUCH FUNCTIONALITY, IS NOT AVAILABLE.

Hence, the prime & primary nature of the fetus now infant, is in the form of a pattern of emotionally based rebellion, a pattern of reactionarism.

The rebel, with or without cause, strikes out, establishing its presence with the affirmation of protest. With rationality, intentional, if unconscious, rebellion & rejection are the 1st intentional affirmations of relationship. A 'habit' is the 1st inheritance of a newly cognitively engaged social entity. The baby rebels 'perfectly.'

Yet, if understood contextually, we must realize that the ultimate NATURAL purpose for which the emotions are to serve is as a part of the central communication & alert system, TO & FOR THE BODY, ITS PERFECT SERVANT, to both establish the something needs attendance, but also emotions serve to act to stress the severity, threat, or other significance that must be noted in the nature of the social response that is needed. Then, rationality & experience come in to play.

Emotions are to play a very transitory role, focused upon impact indicated or that had happened to or in proximity of the body & its interests. They also, depending upon the perception of events, may involve intense responses from the body, everything from chemicals released into the body, pre-determining kinds & qualities of reactions, to movements reactionary, involuntary or intentional. But all in all, the emotions actually are to play a very limited & specific kind & quality of behavioral role.

But, as the 1st stable source for consciousness upon birth, the rational mind too immature & inexperienced to process the flow of events, the emotional dimension allows us to reside unnoticed until either physiological events or events of human meaning intrude. Then awakening to that interpersonal mode of involvement that is more than just acting as a passenger, in a cruising mode, we revert to our comfort zone, our emotional identity, that is the composite of memories selectively inventoried or merely kept for reasons unknown to the conscious mind, until events call them forth. Then, as we examine consciously our living, we allocate emotional response according to a value system never consciously established but is the core of our interpersonal commitment to civility... our conscience.

The emotions are servants to the body... of a very valued nature.

But they are to emerge situationally, responding to stimuli as both physically indicated & as human meaning demands. But... they ONLY exist as a transitory physical interpretation & response to events, that are themselves transitory & thus, NOT emotionally demanding.

Further, to over stimulate the emotions can either or both cause physical damage to the brain or damage to the psyche of the person involved. Obviously, under stimulation, like over stimulation, has its effects, again, the potential being either or both of a physical or psychological nature.

The important point being that emotions are of a transitory nature, they do not inherently involve or demand any moral consideration, for in its role as communicator for the body, the 'moral nature, the environmental nature, the instinct to be employed is beyond the emotions to act upon except to express what is already rationally decided.

The value orientation, the interpersonal civil system of social engagement is the rational element, itself fed by emotionally significant experiences & events. The conscious self gives social context to the public & personal expression of response to experiences, reflecting the level of integrative experiences held & rationally understood for their moral content. This consciousness for the need for integration & also the 'rules' of integration, the requirements to care & be cared about, & the decision to 'care' to the degree possible or any portion thereof, forms the basis for what becomes our conscience.

Hence, the conscience operates as a form of internal law/care center. The distinction being that we may do or not do something merely because we have accepted it should be so or we do not now feel the need to challenge that norm, this in contrast to the 'evolution' of the desire to care that is nurtured itself, for that value, hence, the conscience also acts as the aspect of ourselves that Jesus spoke to when he stated to love our enemy as a stable state of being was to 'act as a child of God", for in the heart offered unconditionally, such a heart moves as God would move amongst humanity.

The challenge… & our historical failure emerges in one context & one only…

We allow our conscious & unconscious self to dwell in the emotional aspect of our identity, separating it from the concerns of the conscience, only as it appeals to the emotions, even in contrast to the nature & natural direction the heart would inform & guide the conscience.

This capacity to choose to 'care' or not & to what degree, is the ultimate & ONLY TRUE FREEDOM HUMANITY UNIQUELY HAS, the benefit of the nature of the rational mind. If we station our identity, as a person & human, under the auspices of the emotions as the deciding & controlling interest, then that quality of emotional maturity will be the deciding moral response.

An extreme example. The young child cannot yet grasp either the significance of life or its loss. If that child holds a gun pointed at another child, having observed such behavior in a movie, without moral context, much beyond the experience & vocabulary & thus rational mind of a child, if this child then kills, it had no foundation for moral reflection, thus, cannot suffer any condemnation, as a judgement before the fact.

The conscience develops with the exposure to interpersonal relationships.

The conscience is the developed awareness of environment… & as a needed guide for any integrative behavior, for the impact it must thus release upon that environment, & other such social actors as may be affected, directly or collaterally. The conscience embodies the various degrees of civil commitment we have made 'to care'. This state of conscience both the effect on us but also signifying our own commitment to interpersonal integration & community.

Maturity is the social measure of the sustainability of our use of our 'conscience' towards the effort & need for interpersonal community & intercourse.

If the foundation for behavior is not socially oriented, if it is anti-social in nature, seeking a sustained state of separation from identity with or integration with community, the 'deviance' is established. This is not to indicate that any kind of punitive response or need for change is immediately indicated, since it is also our conscience that unites us with others, & in this, ML King, Jr not only defended himself, he also spoke for the conscience of all humanity; for the values he reasoned should guide the conscience, were already equally available, & thus as accessible to enemy, as to friend.

King reasoned such values, to inform the human conscience, also defined the human as human.

The challenge created by interpersonal harm is always ultimately rooted in the values that guide & inform our conscience, the measure of our commitment to moral integration. If we allow ourselves an emotional nature, that never evolves beyond self-interest, as it is intended to do with the body, in its defense, then THAT level of public investment will be both the cognitively defined limits as well as those held unconsciously, but emotionally significant.

A child learns the necessity for forgiveness, for the value it serves both to the need for community, & for the stability it brings to oneself in the capacity to not lose oneself to experiences. Hence, the degree of experiences exposed to, understood, incorporated for their 'meaning', the level of vocabulary available for introspection & reflection, all these factors determine the opportunity for maturing that is needed, as we become more experienced, over a broader range of terrain of possibilities for relationship.

The 'evolution' of our emotional maturity is directly proportional to the breadth & quality of interpersonal experiences & values exposed to. But then accepted by oneself, consciously or not. The integration into our capacity & desire to care is what is significant to social outcomes. If our commitment to community & integration is either immature, as we would expect in inexperienced children, or we have not been exposed to a broad enough range of moral paradigms, then our skills at integration & community are going to reflect that disparity.

The challenge in history, for humanity as adults, is that our individual & collective commitment to the issue of the NEED for care as part of the human instinct, is yet haphazard, representing a lack of both genuine care & a constitutional unwillingness to be THAT self-regulating. But the simple truth is… we choose not to care THAT much.

Further, we weren't raised to care THAT much. And…
NO ONE CARED ABOUT US THAT MUCH.

With no living example, no living experience, the path to such a quality of care then is left up to each to struggle with… mostly alone.

Our emotional identity becomes 'god'. WE decide when to be loving, we decide when NOT to be loving… consciously or not, WE ARE NOW GOD.

When we place our emotional identity as ALWAYS LISTENING TO & FOLLOWING THE HEART, THEN THE CONSCIENCE IS OUR FRIEND. IT IS OUR SURROGATE PARENT, GUIDING US TO OUR OWN PARENTHOOD.

If we allow our very essence & desire for relationship to blossom, under the guidance of our conscience, until it becomes our 'habit,' then as Jesus noted, we will be perfect as our parent/father in heaven. If we allow our immature emotions to be the subject of our quality of care offered, then we have allowed the body itself, the emotional part of the brain, never designed to make moral judgments, to reign over the consciousness that has emerged as the crowning statement of the cosmos…

When the creation itself must learn to create, to sustain & justify its own existence.

If not, history is repeated each & every day… Cain kills Abel.

Whom can face their true parent, admitting that they not only killed their sibling, they choose to…because they felt like it…

The 'nature of the cosmos: Inheriting the morally indicated wisdom

Humanity has much opinion… abut itself & about nothing…

Humanity offers many narratives… mostly exulting oneself…

Listening is what women are supposed to be good at… but who wants to be a woman…

What we need to do is REALLY learn to listen…

Then we would discover there is a reality… beyond our mere imagines…

This reality offering its own 'wisdom', hidden between our legs…

That the ONLY means to life, as a sustainable feature of ANYT environment, given its native ecology, is through the means of morally significant, sustainable relationships.

THIS message indicates that a native species emerged not 'born' with a mature instinct, where it seems life has extended a unique opportunity, TO SO PARTICIPATE IN THE CREATION OF SELF, THAT ONE ALSO DETERMINES THE VERY MORAL FABRIC OF THE INTEGRATION NECESSARY, FOR SUCH DIVERSITY OF LIFE TO EMERGE AS A SUSTAINABLE FEATURE…

For humanity, we must access the heart of the matter… that which ONLY in itself will secure the quality of living & life every person naturally seeks, is revealed both in the capacity to recognize & choose the values needed, but also in having the freedom to so act. Acting so, to secure the individual, does so in the only environment capable… when it is occupied & all equally informed with the same quality of commitment to personal, social & political behavior, to integration, & all it implies in the offering of heart.

When we make our capacity to care, our commitment to 'love', to the how of our being with ALL others, then the heart, that capacity to choose to care, to integrate, will truly guide EVERY EMOTIONAL IMPULSE… guiding our emotional engagements from conception to birth, to behavior.

Then love emerges as the guide for all engagement.

We are perfect as our parent/God.

Until then?

Reality as it is.

The individual & social meaning of family: priming the integration pump 'to care'

Christians like to note that even God offers that humanity should consciously participate in the continuation of the species.

Seems the sex life of humans is of cosmic concern.

I guess from a more universal perspective, humanity is informing itself, vis a vis such 'revelations', & through the natural urges that produce offspring as a potential of our engagement of our sexual urges, we are 'encouraged' on all possible fronts to such activity. But the quality of such experience is under our own direct authority.

This is the 1st door to reality.

What quality of integration do we offer to our 'spouse"? What quality of parenting experiences have WE been socialized to & further exposed to? To what personal impact? What values paradigm defined our growing experiences to become adults? What sense of our personal value, as a human, as a unique person? What values & qualities of integration & assimilation did we experience & to what effect? What role did emotions play in the dynamics of relationship & by what values system were the actors assigned roles & individual & social significance?

This all is so defining in the nature of the culture that must then emerge from such families, the next generation of citizens… even if not patriots.

It is thus an intergenerational process & paradigm we honor when we parent.

But… we also accomplish a lot of other socially significant social effects.

Parents introduce us to the reality & personal & social significance of relationships.

In this, parents order our universe. They give it moral meaning, which means our parents introduce us to the importance of 'happiness'.

Parents teach us about rationality, reasoning, allow us to learn the variances of what freedom means, in 'being human', in the quality of civility we integrate to define ourselves to others by. Parents teach us about commitment, citizenship as committed civility, community as the integration of heart. We learn the distinction between love & emotion. Love as motive & behavior beyond self-interest, emotion as the occasion vehicle for a varied expression of love content so interpreted.

Families teach us about repentance… the owning of our failures to love, so that we can then be the authors & architects of our own restorational process & offerings. Hence, in forgiving us, in this guidance back to community, we discover the living value of love translated situationally.

It is in this environment, with this committed standard of the surrounding environment & its actors, that we experience…

The True Family Values… the "science" of life & living… designed & 'created' specifically for human consumption

Book 4

The civil promise made to... the world

Securing the Homeland: The 1st civil right & patriots as the living wisdom of a nation

(The affirmation of self as 'WE are,' because I am, to you, as you are, to me)

"... I have longed to hear white ministers say, "Follow this decree because integration is morally RIGHT & the Negro is your brother." M.L. King, Jr.

"History in its pure form furnishes no value by itself." Albert Camus

"A philosophical attempt to work out a universal history of the world in accord with a plan of nature that aims at a perfect civic union of the species must be regarded as possible & even helpful to this objective of nature." Kant

"Rules & formulas, those mechanical aids to the rational use, or rather misuse, of his natural gifts, are the shackles of a permanent immaturity." Kant

"... the supreme end of man's vocation, sociability." Kant
"You must not hate your brother in your heart... You must not take vengeance or bear a grudge against the children of

your people, but you must love your neighbor as yourself. I am the Lord." Leviticus 19:17-18

My/our 1st challenge: reconfiguring our value system as to what & how we define "homeland".

There is a generation of difference between a country that offers the same civil rights we observe in the American version, with its defining morally significant initial 4 word imperative & the reality of the same rights offered under a dictatorship, of an ideologically driven individual or nation or a dictatorship of one.

So often, as a lecturer for an educational program to confront Marxism & other forms of communism, I remarked that the saving grace in America was that there was no forced atheism or societal attack against religion. Further, I erringly, in common with so many others, touted America as a 'Christian' nation.

Oh, the innocence of ignorance.

And the social harms it then enables, for the lack of any meaningful protest on my part.

Was I even paying attention?

Ever since its founding, religion & religious people have been under attack in America... ALL PERPETRATED BY 'CHRISTIANS'...

Hence, the 'version' of Jesus they offered was... well, wrong.

A litany of examples? Witches plague the powerless people & a threat to be eliminated, Catholics bother people for their divided loyalty, hence must be persecuted, Christian & Jew cannot be imagined to embrace the same one, true God, thus Jews MUST be persecuted. Muslims are totally a historical fanatical circus act, in the eyes of American Christians, & thus, disparaged & hounded on every front, EVERY Muslim responsible for the sins of the few. Unlike Christians, ALWAYS FORGIVEN, NO MATTER WHAT, OUR WHITE GOD

BEING THE SUPERIOR GOD. Hindus, Buddhists are/were the laughing stock of such Americans. Now, 'all' Muslims are terrorists or at least absolute supporters of terrorism. 'Cults' almost destroyed America until Christians stepped in & started kidnapping members off the streets of America, & then holding them in forced isolation, without legal representation or consultation, deprogramming them. Black America still has not learned its proper place, demonstrations ALL deemed a form of ungrateful rioting, by an equally ungrateful Black populace, for the freedoms they do have. Trump took credit for keeping such people OUT OF THE SUBURBS, SAVING THEIR NEIGHBORHOODS FROM A BLACK ONSLAUGHT OF POOR PEOPLE, MOVING INTO THEIR SACRED NEIGHBORHOODS.

So, if the KKK & other such white terrorist hate groups could & can exist in America, even flourish, arrogantly touting their anti-Constitutional values & yet not have their rhetoric challenged, even by a sitting president, as in opposition to the Constitution & Bill of Rights, where was MY protest? If the continued killing of black Americans could proceed unhindered, & continues to happen, where was MY protest? When they invoked the name of Jesus or God, to support racism & sexism & environmental sacrilege, where was the universal protest of Christian ministry? Who then defended Jesus or God? What Christian defended the creation, the home a gift from God? Where is stewardship & covenant?

Further, & this is REALLY the crux of the matter, if the Constitution stipulates to a human reasoned conclusion about the universal state of humanity, what is MY personal, public & political obligation?

This rationally held & shared conclusion, offered in four founding words, about the nature of the individuals who will thus inhabit this particular nation, under such declared auspices & authorized as a founding declaration, thus are to be given such consideration, by every person seeking the benefits offered as rights of socially significant behavior, that EVERY person, to receive such benefit, offers to the community that equal protection. When, as a community, individuals that have so integrated the significance of the individual as the foundation for all interpersonal activity, then that community offers the ONLY TRUE SACRED VENUE FOR LIVING, AS A HUMAN. Such integration of an essential value, reasoned as the ONLY means to a universal suffrage for EVERY individual, establishes their own claim most perfectly when they honor, in behavior, the living witness as to the meaning & value thus assigned the individual, this also no less the will of the people who were so deprived in history.

Such declaration, considered in the context of the history that demanded such a nation emerge, & in the context of the now sought to be protected values & social behaviors, then demands such civility that ALL then can share in the protected 'bounty' of civil rights.

If there is a founding value that defined the limits & boundaries of freedom, American or human, the 4 included words offer the perfect logic to a compelling authority (WE, humans, so choose that observation as our North Star,) as to HOW such rights would be protected, by all, & for all. Based upon such authority, as socially significant inequities came to light, so morally compelling so as to be commonly recognized as needing remedying, the Supreme Court has been saddled, many times in its history, to give once more a reigning definition, in living application, of the personal, public & political significance & coinage of the realm as impacted by those few words.

Those words rationally justified the end of slavery, if not the unchristian values that had informed & sought to justify evil as also 'God's' will. Those four words demanded the vote be properly offered to all. On & on, humanity has had to defend what all knew all along that was wrong, but figured better to assume heaven's forgiveness than lose an opportunity for meaning for the imagined profit it realized, even if evil in its source.

Thus, reviewing American history, who has been the defender of the people, who has taken up the banner for the full implementation of those four words? Well, 1st & foremost was the Constitution itself. In its defense of itself.

2nd, to defend THAT Constitution, women, men & women, minorities, all stood before their counterparts, arguing that America was being used to betray the people it was created to serve.

Yet, even today, Christians demand the 'right' to hate whom they will hate, the Constitution somehow protecting such behavior. They don't have to love anyone, for they are Christians & they assume thus any mistakes they make are already forgiven. (Jesus has already had the last word on that, but no one seems to read Jesus' own words anymore. Well, the mean words anyway...)

I have only one moral response to that human reasoned declaration... as to the 'protected' right to hate whomever one chooses.

If your God sanctions such shit, then may that God suffer the same hell created for such entities, as promised. Because those who so indulge such values were uniformly declared evil by Jesus & assured a seat NOT WITH GOD.

So, why in the hell did these men decide to include this most onerous of inclusions & declarations?

The 1st rationale was self-serving.

They acted to defend themselves & their personal interests, which, for once in history, also established the opportunity to offer a universal value & social awareness to a potential of quality of civil union never before imagined on such a scale.

This is the wisdom, that they offered, in self-interest, but with some vision as to its potential for instigating righteous rebellion... to end slavery, to **return** the right to vote. To inhibit & stop various forms of unchristian discrimination, practiced & forced upon others by Christians.

The 1st wisdom then the inclusion of those fated words.

Jesus offered that the true child of God, did the will of God. Hence, to ANY wannabe Christian, the 1st challenge to his faith is his neighbor. You know, the one we don't like. America demands we NOT forget ourselves & NOT love our neighbor, that guy who is also equal to me. If I limit his pleasurable & reasonable access to the civil rights that define MY universe, then am I treating him equally? Am I acting in the zone Jesus stated would establish my lineage to Jesus, & thus, God?

Jesus did warn pretenders though. Warned they were not qualified to be anything but the trash needing to be taken out.

Only fools attempt to make what is, into what is not, nor can be.

Or, as evidenced by the state of mind that morally tries to justify hate, we will exhibit we are pathologically inclined by free will to mental illness & deviance.

So, as American history offers so poignantly, citizens may not carry the celebration of that 1st demanded social consideration, AS citizens, into their living. Instead offering. AS we observe, & as we experience, such emotionally defined behaviors that are more naturally expected & more recognizable in unruly children.

However, such citizens not allowing such principles to educate & challenge us to a heart to heart integration, as Jesus demands, we MUST ASSERT such citizens could still offer such civility that the experience of others to such protected community & behaviors is not hindered nor diminished & aborted. But then we end up back to the question as to 'why' we have to treat others equally.

Ever notice that the ones who NEVER value a moral stance, never allow that it is THEY who should suffer such diminished social civility?

Treat a white person as less than human? Perish the thought!!! THEY, we must note, don't DESERVE such treatment... therefore, the conclusion being that the rest DO DESERVE such treatment.

But, human will, even to embrace evil, demanded as some right, is the news EVERY day for women, racial, religious & ethnic communities... & the environment, awaiting the revealing of the 'sons of man'.

The line in the sand that delineates then the patriot from the citizen, as a morally significant counter point, is the degree of living defense those 4 words hold as a socially compelling public mind & conscience, in our emotional commitments & behavioral expressions.

The nation needed, needs those words, to defend what was not, is not yet celebrated universally. Not yet even celebrated in America, so few true patriots in evidence in leadership. Even though the people beg.

Honor the 1st truth; the universal & sacred value of all life, with no natural entitlements to be offered nor declared. The world needs these same values defended universally. Hence, the living social significance of a nation that can create the ultimate witness to the power, viability & value of such a socially defined political human system.

Yet, today, where is our true moral American human leadership? Where is the heart of Americans? Where is the evidence of our public mind, our social conscience"?

Calling racists 'good' people?

Treating women as 'property'?

Cheating people out of debts?

Creating charities to make profit for oneself?

Create businesses that cheat others as its prime goal? Its entitlement?

Treating people of color as less than human, that view guiding all moral considerations?

Imagining ONLY Christianity as suited to America?

Imagining America must be held by white people & the wealthy, who then can squeeze all for any profit to be made? Be damned the future & any impact? On America OR the world?

Truth: ONLY true Americans, living by that 1st civil principle, can guarantee each other the proper quality of experience of the Bill of Rights, to truly give the witness that we understand the history that demanded those words & this nation, to give witness to the celebration of beloved community it naturally encourages… & the hope it offers to the world.

The patriot is the citizen who understands the history that demanded such a nation, defending such values, declaring them fit to all humanity, to the least.

The patriot, in such effort, offers wisdom disguised as behavior. The patriot offers the quality of humility that defines the hero…when the only vision is the inclusive one, that defines

& defends all as sacred, one no less than another, even to our enemy.

The patriot realizes that a nation that defends an 'all' this way, also defends all others, in all other countries, as intrinsically also sharing such a value.

This then requires such international discourse that words are used ONLY to serve the greater purpose, the moral movement of humanity to a state that can create & sustain beloved community.

THAT NO LESS WAS & IS THE POTENTIAL OF AMERICA... PROVIDED THE CITIZEN SO DECIDES THE VISION OF AMERICA IS ALSO THEIR VISION, THEIR WAY OF LIFE, OFFERING THEIR WAY OF LIVING, WITH EACH TO THE OTHER.

How else to protect a nation, & a nation to protect its people, then when each citizen comes to make such personal, public & political commitment, that like the Jews, to be Jewish was to be of a moral commitment of a particular quality with all other Jews. To be American, 4 words thus inspire us to express the pride of patriotism, to carry forth the banner the defines the unique value of this nation, to itself no more than to the world. Values ONLY given witness in the celebration of community... that honors as its 'cause celebre' the very values that MOST challenge the globe in its moral demand for universal suffrage & attendance to such absolute values. Such values that then defend EVERY human no less than ANY other.

Recognizing the universal social significance of morally significant sustained communities, the patriot, of ANY nation, then acts as a universal patriot. THAT patriot recognizes no sovereignty as truly legitimate that denies such fundamental values to its people. No people so held against their will should be ignored, for their race, religion, ethnicity. Are such governing bodies somehow therefore exempt from such personal, public & political expressions as to offer contrast & moral exception to their own immoral values?

Such evidence of values held & offered in behavior, by the patriot, as the final measure of both our commitment to self-love as well as the full measure of our commitment to the values that naturally define all life, each to the other, are the final & ONLY absolute defense of that nation.

Here is the security of a nation secured.

Here is a nation defended, a form of love defended, in the ONLY measure meaningful, a socially engaged integration. this by the true patriot.

A defense of nation, of neighbor, of self, offered in the blood, sweat & tears of living, not dying.

A security established in the definition of self that engages all, that thus integrates, as a matter of heart, with all.

There is no greater wisdom, no greater security offered to a nation, than a people who are so defined by their living. By the nature of the commitment they have offered one another, & in the nature of the values defined & offered in behavior? That commitment to a universal wisdom & security is then established.

Today, the true patriot is the last defense for the unique, absolute value of the individual, to themselves, but only fully realized in beloved community. Are we willing?

Civil rights vs religious rights: Accepting the morally demanded limits of political social action between church & state

(The maturity of recognizing & accepting morally significant limits to freedom, to impose upon others)

"I am coming to feel that the people of ill will have used time much more effectively than the people of good will." M.L. King, Jr.

"Let us be dissatisfied until every state capitol houses a governor who will do justly, who will love mercy & who walk humbly with his God." M.L. King, Jr.

"Did not Moses give you the law, & yet none of you keepth the law? Why go ye about to kill me?" Jesus

For Americans, there is a 1st principle; religious rights are a 2nd tier morally significant behavior, given articulation & defense as a 'civil' right. Civil rights refer to all the behaviors, rhetorical as well as actual, that are defined or defended in a particular community. Behaviors that are defined as morally significant community norms. Hence, behaviors to be shared, in common, in their engagement.

I observed/suffered America in the last days as it sought to decide whom should be 'hired' as the next national manager for America.

I also observed two distinct power centers & voting blocks that supported Trump. The makeup & social arrogance of these two, in actuality antagonistic life styles that are actually opposed to each other. Yet, in the end, your enemy is my enemy, hence, we are united.

One major group are those who especially nurture the quality of values that engages, integrates & celebrates, in behavior, the moral context of Trump's own thrust towards those to whom he has either issues with or otherwise have no compunction to respect or otherwise entertain any civil notions about. These people Trump himself ultimately has no respect for, even as he manipulates them into emotional furies more reminiscent of children throwing temper tantrums. These are the people that are part of Trump in no way in his normal life, only serving at best as employees, they beneath his own stature & personal, social & political position. The nationalists & racists are 'kin' only in the context of a shared dislike & disrespect for others. Hence, the secularists that support Trump ONLY are pawns to him, a means to an ends. For him.

His promise sheet does not measure up to his promises, ever. It cannot. But, it is always someone else who is responsible

Trump not only has no sense of genuine care for others, he is a racist & thus, also attracts that element that shares not only his brashness & incivility, they also share his hate of others.

Between those who want to blame someone for all the wrongs they imagine has been done to them, as 'deserving' & 'exceptional' Americans, those who share this but are racists & nationalists, & 'those blue collar who support his attitudes towards women & minorities & the rich, they all became part of a 'cult' phenomena that has not been so observed up close since the "Heaven's Gate" suicide & Jim Jones Jonestown murder/suicide massacre.

Trump's group, to belong, knew they had to embrace the whole package. It's anarchistic self-indulgence of everything emotional, in behavior & rhetoric, became everything we imagine children are to be chastised for & corrected. Trump encouraged & allowed a degree of uncivil values to emerge that reflected the very values that created, sustained & sought to legitimize racism & sexism.

That these people so hate America that their own personal struggles, at this time in history, encourages & justifies such incivility argues that the family traditions of community, civility & citizenship were dissolved. Long before Trump appeared.

He is rather the consummate capitalist. He will use ANY resources, FOR ANY PURPOSE, IF IT SUITS HIS OWN WILL & DESIRES, INCLUDING & ESPECIALLY USING PEOPLE & THEIR RESOURCES. Money, muscle or mind, what serves Trump is Trump's NATURAL RIGHT TO DEMAND.

What is critical to note, that in the rhetoric & behavior of Trump are expressed the values that drive, guide & inform his very essence. Trump is anti-social to the extreme & allows not dissent. Where American standards of civility demand an allowance for community & hence, community values that encourage & support integration, Trump had no such desire. His way or no way. (He actually embodies what social scientists now label as the 'dark side' of human nature, which is in all actuality the values of the anti-social pathologically driven individual. He embraces every one of the offered & defined characteristics…)

THAT value orientation to rule ALL decisions.

Trump, communists, fascists, Nazi's, pedophiles, murderers, capitalists, Christians; ALL WORSHIP THE SAME GOD… THE ONE THAT ALLOWS HATE OF OTHERS.

THEN, we have the question of the Christian vote.

MILLIONS OF CHRISTIANS WERE MISLED, LED BY A CHRISTIAN LEADERSHIP THAT OFFERED A RELIGIOUS INTERPRETATION OF TRUMP, HIS SIGNIFICANCE TO GOD, AMERICA & AMERICANS, & THE WORLD.

These millions were led to believe that Trump's birth was preordained. That God created Trump to save America &

serve as the Middle East messiah to save Israel from her enemies.

HENCE, CHRISTIANS, MILLIONS OF PROTESTANT, CONSERVATIVE CHRISTIANS WERE LED TO BELIEVE THAT THE ONLY WAY TO SERVE GOD, TO BE UNITED WITH GOD, WAS TO VOTE FOR & SUPPORT TRUMP.

This age group was by & large over 50 years old.

But it included many millions of families, led to believe THEY, & ONLY THEY, BY VOTING FOR TRUMP, SERVED GOD, COUNTRY & THE WORLD JESUS IS YET TO RECLAIM.

Such Christian leadership also argued that interracial marriage was Satanic... & such was being advanced by Communist countries for Americans as a way to destroy America from within.

This is a nationally advanced idea...millions now believe it, for they fear anything labeled 'communist' so much, that the use of the word itself is enough to introduce emotional irrationality & fear...

YET NOT ONE CHURCH, NOT ONE RELIGION, NOT ONE POLITICAL GROUP, NOT ONE DECRIED SUCH UNAMERICAN IDEAS...

What happened to "ALL... ARE CREATED EQUAL"?

Where is the civility that America demands, so that the celebration of civil rights that America articulates & defends, may be offered to all, as it was ALWAYS INTENDED.

Given Trumps own values, he is 100% unsuited to lead a nation, much less a family.

That Republicans didn't care?

The measure of Republican love for the nation... & all her people.

That he offered the right 'buzz' words, like anti-abortion, economy (of which was recovering nicely as he was elected... lest we forget), anti-communism, anti-socialist (though he believes in socialism for the rich, that they can get richer) & anti-immigrant (read racist).

When Trump offered a 'SMALL' tax relief for the average America that year, he offered himself, as a 'rich' person & as a corporation owner, 2 tax breaks that meant millions for him & those like him.

THAT TAX BREAK FOR THE WEALTHIEST & CORPORTATIONS CONTINUES YEAR TO YEAR... BUT ONLY FORF THEM.

IN THE MEANTIME, TAX MONEY THAT HAD BEEN USED TO PAY OUR NATIONAL BILLS, HAVE BEEN ADDED TO OUR NATIONAL BILL.

WHILE TRUMP, THE RICH LIKE HIM, & CORPORATIONS? ALL REJOICE IN THE SIMPLE AMERICAN MIND...

You want an example where religion has assumed rights not in evidence? How & why Christians voted for Trump.

MISLED BY A CHRISTIAN LEADERSHIP NEVER UNDERSTOOD JESUS, HIS WORDS & MISSION, NOR THE GOD JESUS SOUGHT TO DEFEND. TODAY, NO CHRISTIAN IN AMERICA TRULY KNOWS THE ORIGIANAL JESUS, THE JESUS THAT WOULD NEVER ALLOW A TRUMP TO LEAD ANYTHING, OR ANYONE.

TRUMP IS THE ANTITHESIS OF EVERYTHING JESUS LIVED & DIED TO PROTECT.

PAUL WARNED CHRISTIANS NEVER TO ASSOCIATE WITH SUCH PEOPLE, TO OFFER JUDGMENT TO THEM, TO SAVE THEM.

YET, THEY THINK TRUMP WAS SENT BY GOD TO SAVE US?

ONLY IF TRUMP & THE CURRENT CHRISTIAN GOD IS SATAN...

For Christians to vote for Trump?

It seated evil/Satan in the most powerful seat in the world... that is the Christian understanding of Jesus... there is none.

Hence, EVERYTHING CHRISTIANS ARGUE FOR THIS NATION, MUST BE SUSPECT. EXAMINED WITHIN THE CONTEXT OF... "ALL... are created equal" & therefore, entitled to the same quality of civil rights.

This election established clearly the danger of unbridled religious belief being used as the measure for civil & civic action, including voting.

This election demonstrates EXACTLY HOW A GROUP, WITH ENOUGH SOCIAL POWER, CAN MANIPULATE THE COURSE OF A NATION, AWAY FROM ITS OWN FOUNDING & DEFENDED PRINCIPLES... WHEN WE, THE PEOPLE, ONLY CARE FOR OURSELVES, & NOT THE NATION & WORLD WE AHRE WITH OTHERS.

BUT WILL WE LEARN.

TRUMP IS COMING BACK IN 2024... ARE WE READY?

The people who supported him, are still here.

With the same values & religious ideas...

Here is a listing of the 'D-Factor', the dark side of human nature. It is the perfection of the anarchist who also chooses NOT to care about others. Thus, the behaviors are anti-social in nature & result in all the varieties of human harm we are yet to master. This list appeared in an article by Scott Barry Kaufman, The Dark Core of Personality.

The Actual *D*-Factor: These are the nine traits that comprised their *D*-factor:

. *Egoism.* The excessive concern with one's own pleasure or advantage at the expense of community well-being.

. *Machiavellianism.* Manipulativeness, callous affect, and strategic-calculating orientation.

. *Moral Disengagement.* A generalized cognitive orientation to the world that differentiates individuals' thinking in a way that powerfully affects unethical behavior.

. **Narcissism.** An all-consuming motive for ego-reinforcement.

5. **Psychological Entitlement.** A stable and pervasive sense that one deserves more and is entitled to more than others.
6. **Psychopathy:** Deficits in affect, callousness, self-control, and impulsivity.
7. **Sadism.** Intentionally inflicting physical, sexual, or psychological pain or suffering on others in order to assert power and dominance or for pleasure and enjoyment.
8. **Self-Interest.** The pursuit of gains in socially valued domains, including material goods, social status, recognition, academic or occupational achievement, and happiness.
9. **Spitefulness.** A preference that would harm another but that would also entail harm to oneself. This harm could be social, financial, physical, or an inconvenience.

These are the characteristics of the man Christian America imagined God demanded, to save America. That IF THEY DID NOT VOTE THEN FOR HIM, THEY WERE THEREFORE AGAINST GOD'S WILL, & THUS, AGAINST GOD... HOW LONG WOULD SUCH PEOPLE PREVAIL AGAINST SUCH COMPELLING IMAGERY & ETERNAL THREATS?

Further, the Christian churches involved have EVEN GONE SO FAR AS TO DECLARE, WITHOUT TRUE AUTHORITY, TO DECLARE THAT TRUMP'S VERY PRESIDENCY IS CRITICAL TO THE RETURN OF JESUS AT THIS TIME OF HISTORY.

With such a RELIGIOUS imperative, American religion if reversing the course of the development of freedom, a freedom shared by all, dictated by none, invested in as a matter of family principles, applied to the need for social civility & community.

Yet, what defense does America have against such an emotionally driven onslaught?

Remember 1st principles & thus, that in all being created equal, in America, one's religious interpretation of life & its influences cannot be applied as binding to all others.

2nd, & this is the pivot point, the true & absolute standard taught by Jesus, as ONLY being the BEHAVIOR OF THE

FAITHFUL needs to be resurrected & restored to the people… all the people.

Without such clarity, such 'Christians' cannot properly judge what their leaders are offering as the teachings Jesus sought to be inherited, even by the least.

Without such clarity, such people cannot truly know either the will of God, nor how that is acted out on a secular level, as we live, with each other. They cannot understand the significance of 4 words, the providential potential of the nation they abide in, through no real effort of their own.

When we come to assume an entitlement, based upon birth, then we repeat all the worst of history, that America was created to confront, to inspire change within & without, from the individual, to the family, to the nation. A nation of mutually acknowledged equals.

Equals for the labors to sustain the nation, equals to the benefits it creates, including from such natural resources that are the proper inheritance of all humanity, for all time.

Or we are no Christian nation.

Which, when all is tallied, is really NOT the right distinction for a nation that offers at its founding defining value, that "ALL… are created equal."

Better it be said that in America, Christians HONOR the words, message & mission of Jesus, as HE dictated it, not as it has been reinterpreted. But, when the sun sets, America is a nation of religious & those not religious.

In this opportunity, EVERY citizen is the anchor for all others.

Rhetoric IS behavior: The 'I & thou' of loving my enemy, as a citizen, in the times of confrontation

(I honor myself in what I offer to others... the justified exceptionalism)

"Let me rush on to mention my other disappointment. I have been so greatly disappointed with the white church & its leadership... I say it as a minister of the gospel, who loves the church..." M.L. King, Jr.

"Set your mind on God's kingdom & his justice before everything else..." Jesus

"What I meant to say..."

You notice how seldom the word 'nigger' crosses the lips of white people these days? Is this evidence of an evolving integration & standard of civility in even the most racist white? Or is it merely the civil behavior that is to be given, as a demand?

Or is it, that to so engage another, today, does not offer the same social support; but rather, even in this limited racist society, freely offered hate-filled rhetoric does pose significant risk to self, as it did not under a forced terrorist system of apartheid?

Today, black anger has finally been owned.

Oh, yes, baby, it is scary.

Why?

Maturing of the masses?

Enlightenment?

A sense of needed repentance?

The owning of the past, as still being the present & thus, needing repentance?

Naw... now for once, if you assault a black person verbally, they need not so fear the Southern black-tie party as they once did. Today, black America may return barb for barb. If one pursues such avenues too enthusiastically, they just might get their ass appropriately kicked into next week.

Hmmm... seems that rhetoric is a VERY socially significant 'behavior'.

Yet, even weekly some new fake Christian, assuming for a 'right' the anarchy of the spoiled child, that must mature to accept the need for sharing the playground, is paraded before us for the personal, public & political abuse they subjected another citizen to. Then? Applauded by other juveniles for the abuse of America's core values, it still is imagined as we are protected in our choices to act like an ass; but, then people rush to complain when black America returns in kind... on their streets, instead of directly on their person.

I am not advocating violence by black America as a social response. But then, to be honest, one MUST EXPECT RIGHTEOUS ANGER... YOU WOULD BE, TOO. IF YOU WERE HUMAN

Yes, I am stipulating to the 'fact' that the human member of the species is not only endowed with the capacity to care, that if such moral consideration is not integral to one's essential nature & social behavioral norms, then we will observe the pathologically inclined deviant. Then we have a Trump-type personality.

Is it significant to the leadership of a healthy nation if its president scores a perfect 10 for fully engaging ALL the anti-social, 'dark personality' characteristics noted by social scientists? Especially if in EVERY way, they also violate the 1st civil right & social obligation established by the Constitution itself? (Rhetorical question, for those who support Trump...)

Logic further offers the rational conclusion that unless such uncivil characteristics were hidden from the public, which they weren't & are not, instead paraded as an 'up yours!' entitlement, then the people who elected him to represent a supposedly Christian nation, must be questioned as to their own psychological health. Much less their moral & ethical education & health.

The anti-social pathology identified by social scientists as the 'dark side' of human nature, is actually a judgment on the characteristics that DO NOT SUPPORT human INTEGRATION; ESPECIALLY DEVOID OF ANY DESIRE & SOCIAL EXPRESSION OF THE HUMAN CAPACITY TO CARE, BEYOND SELF-INTEREST, OR TO OTHERWISE EXPRESS 'HEART', as it affects our universal & individual need for human meaning, realized ONLY through integration & community.

In identifying such behaviors, as indicating a missing of morally significant social commitment to human community, a universally recognized need, even if human behavior does not honor the wisdom offered as such, we again establish the priority of universal human need, that the creation of America was to provide remedy for. But 'freedom' is selfishly decided by such people as a privately held special entitlement. Hence, the continuing need for the sexual & civil suits that become demanded, if not yet honored; still advanced for the time when at least a significant social judgment may emerge on America's values, as currently interpreted & acted out.

Such unprincipled behavior defended when an administration informs the world, "It's America, bitch!" The underbelly of immaturity that saturates this nation today was celebrated that day. A day needing repentance.

When we encounter such values, such use of human freedom, or actually misuse, we touch the root of all human harm. The will to NOT care…

But the days of such racist 'freedom', properly read this as anarchy, those days of absolute impunity & arrogance must be dispensed with, gone, even with White House support for such values. ONLY when given the support, translate given power & authority, of civil police, local & national governmental servants & their biased judges, does racism continue to reign, as a value held by some who claim citizenship. Such racism existing because of apathy, a significant lack of self-love & embracing self-serving, anti-social values & thus, the lack of a true commitment to universal civil rights. Denying the sustainable creation of such interpersonal moral standards any community needs to establish the quality of civility that creates not only beloved community, but a national identity to challenge any in the world for its natural psychological health.

What happens when we encourage hate as a right of citizenship?

Do we REALLY imagine that the white cop beating a black citizen, with the barest of resistance being offered, rhetorically much less physically, is not THINKING 'nigger'? FEELING 'nigger'?

Can we understand that we have created a society where a 'black' cop can FEEL 'nigger' towards other black folk BECAUSE the racism is so systemic that to be a black cop can also translate into NOT being black on the job. Then, even other black Americans can be reduced to simple stereotypes, on an emotional level, where the worst damage to relationships emerge.

Hell, it's how I feel towards such white people. I admit, I am yet to love my enemy. Because of such white people & their values & social behaviors, to me, THEY ARE THE TRUE NIGGERS, if such a thing could exist. They defile our nation, making sure our country is hell & only becoming worse. Such Christians are the NEW GODLESS AMERICANS, just like their Marxist hate-filled equals. If I could ship such people off to some country more worthy of their values, maybe off-planet, I admit, I might be tempted. Not EVERYONE will be restored in their lifetime.

Nor should they be allowed to destroy a nation, even in the name of Jesus. But how do we educate whom would NOT be educated? How do we integrate such people into the greater whole? How do we love an enemy, who hates not because it is right to do so, but because they choose to. Whom seeks to enslave, is less than ANY slave. For the slave is not acting as a morally significant social agent so as to act as an anarchist, rather than as a citizen.

Since there is no such thing as a 'nigger', never was, then the ONLY people worthy of such a designation, given its implied & asserted meanings, & founding values, are those who use the term in its hate-filled form.

The ONLY REAL NIGGERS IN AMERICA MUST THEREFORE BE SUCH WHITES AS SEEK TO USE THE TERM, TO HURT, TO HARM & DENIGRATE OTHERS.
IT IS THEIR OWN BEHAVIORS THAT JUDGE THEM AS THE EQUAL TO THE TERM. SEMI-HUMAN.

If the 'lessor' human is the question before us, from an evolutionary point of view or merely human reasoned, the pathological & antisocial nature of the pathology of racism establishes such people as the 'deviant', the more 'retarded' human. The human needing to mature in their understanding about the nature of ALL life & the corresponding needs of humanity, as individuals & humanity in toto. Just as a family educates for the moral needs to exist & flourish as a family, so too the national level 'family' has moral 'needs', to exist much less to prosper.

If we must assume, finally, that the species, in its current moral climate, is NOT acting as a mature family would, in its cumulative self-interest, then time is of the essence. The numbers of such cultural & racial deviants is not the significant variable here. The people's social awareness as to the value, human need for & the cosmic significance of interpersonal, sustainable, relationships is.

There has never been an American presidential race in which I, & all America, did not observe not only inhospitable rants & raves about & between the individuals & their respective parties.

But it was not until I was forced to stop being a Republican, for the values that the right wing now supported & why, that I began a whole re-evaluation as to what my ultimate & true values are or should be.

Then, the whole focus of my rhetoric changed.

But not replaced with a 'niceness' meant to indicate love, but actually a form of forced personal space, 'civil' considerations inclining towards accepting such effort as the 'real' thing. It is not.

To 'truly' care about others, in passing, in social engagement, in politically sensitive & charged environments, I discovered that the values that Jesus demanded, that would thus also naturally fulfill my obligation/opportunity as a citizen to my neighbor,

"All... are created equal": The natural & Constitutional limits placed upon the Bill of Rights

(We exist as 'sacred' individuals in a protected collective because of 'how' we are with each other)

("(the black man) has no rights which the white man is bound to respect..." *Dred Scott vs Sandford*)

"On the other hand, you know, you got to be honest about what it means to lead a country, it means killing people." Tucker Carlson shared during a phone call on "Fox & Friends"

It is intellectually, rationally & morally revealing that Americans, especially white Christian America, do not yet understand the limits on freedom, that America naturally demands of her mature citizenship, but to which Jesus ALSO speaks to.

Jesus offers American Christians even a more exacting commitment, to both citizenship... & to what it means to be a human, as a child of God, as one who professes 'faith' in Jesus & the words of life that defined him as the global & universally social significant agent he is. Even to this day. Not some god, not as some entity beyond the scope of human experience, but a human, being merely, but truly, human,

Further, as Christians, as the benefactors of the 'words' that free human imagination to recognize our true potential,

Christians are betraying not only Jesus, but God, & finally, & critically, their behavior has degraded the average experience of integration & civility America promises is the inheritance of all, to be shared with all.

In the living failure of American white Christians to not only defend Jesus & God to the world, they have denied others the very love Christians claim for themselves.

This is the MOST egregious of denied behaviors, for there is no greater need in humanity than both an understanding of the personal significance to the lack of genuine care in the world, but also to what it means to generating the quality of civility Jesus & God demands as the moral normative investment of self into community.

Hence, with white Christian Americans refusing to honor Jesus, his words, his God, then there is no witness to Jesus or God in the world. Teaching ABOUT Jesus is not to offer the living Jesus.

Jesus would not recognize the teachings & rhetoric being offered in churches & on TV. Most now serve as the foundation for the 'anti-Christ' to propagate false teachings, about Jesus, God & Trump.

Jesus said to love your enemy.

The leader of America MUST understand those words, live those words, or he cannot be imagined to serve God, Jesus or nation. For what will not serve Jesus nor God, will not serve the interests of a nation, declared Christian or not.

But there is no God in America anymore. We have forced God out. There is no room for either Jesus or God in Christian America.

If we honor all are created equal, then we realize racism is wrong. When we honor all are created equal, we recognize sexism as wrong. When we love God, we realize & recognize that the 'creation' is not just something to be used, abused & discarded as it suits us. There is a moral responsibility for proper stewardship.

All of this MUST be considered & integrated into our being, into our way of being, with all others, EVEN BEFORE WE IMAGINE TO ENGAGE THE CIVIL RIGHTS THAT WE THEN MUST SHARE WITH ONE ANOTHER.

For how we honor those 4 words will immediately determine HOW we interpret & act upon those protected behaviors, with others. To experientially establish that value as a fact among men & women, or to redefine its meaning, hence, deny its meaning & social & political intent.

When a nation, among nations, make such a declaration that ALL humanity, not ONLY those within the confines of a territory, that ALL humanity is to be accepted as 'created equal', by nature or nature's God, that nation has established several socially significant declarations.

If ALL are created equal, then ANY nation that does not honor such a rational prescription for how we must initially engage one another, as equals, then that nation has not protected its people in such form. Hence, in the natural & rational limitations such a universal declaration establishes, it is not only within the natural right of purview to then also conclude that ALL nations should honor such a value, it should be expected.

But only offered to the world in the corresponding witness its own people offer.

There cannot REALLY be Option A, Option B, etc. There IS ONLY ONE RATIONAL STANDARD… however you source its creation.

Then, once we have established the national/global standard, we ALL clearly understand the natural implications. If we all share the same value, as even nature itself would define it, then the moral implication offers that we need to match our public, interpersonal & political behaviors to match that expectation.

How we achieve the needed psychological & emotional state needed to recognize the national level 'created' morally significant designation, so that our civil behavior reflects that common commitment, is a matter left for the use of the protected behaviors articulated in the Bill of Rights.

Freedom of religion allows us that avenue of moral reflection. So does any rational examination of human history. Understanding the primal significance of morally significant sustainable relationships, as the key to life, its sustainability & diversity, allows even the atheist the same quality of material for reflection.

Hence, even before we enter the arena of social behavior, each person, citizen or not, has the morally significant opportunity to translate just how they will justify what behavior they will now offer others. Hence, the Christian is left with the words of Jesus. The Jew, the Torah. The 2 Great Commandments. The atheist, well, we have the witness of the cosmos as to the ONLY needed wisdom & which offers the quality of authority that cannot be ignored... except by the fool.

I have acted as a fool.

But no fool stands before you today.

Every people have understood discrimination, a tempering of sociality when people have a bias that affects interpersonal potential for relationships. But, because of this quality of interpersonal 'priming', we also understand how wrong it is when we act with bias.

America's founders reveal either a wisdom, or an intuitive wisdom, when they opted to include those 4 foundational words. Yet, it was also the justification to argue against a form of forced authority for which they had no possible response... except rebellion.

Yet, those words would foretell the eventual conflict that would emerge, when what was now relatively new, became a national habit, legitimized through the non-confrontational apathetic willingness to leave to the future what they knew was wrong now. Thus, ALL were NOT EQUAL under the laws allowed.

There can be no way to offer this was an innocent oversight. The reason the issue of slavery was argued was because of the ethical & moral arguments surrounding its practice, much less even the idea. Thus, moral reasoning was sufficient to allow any REASONABLE & RATIONAL person to determine, with the limited logics of the times, to still reason slavery is wrong. Why?

Is ANYONE truly willing to subject themselves to such treatment? Then, THAT consensus offers the viewpoint that CANNOT BE IGNORED.

If all are equal, yet no one would subject themselves to the experiences of slavery history reveals was the norm, then ALL have determined such social intercourse is universally wrong.

Yet, if slavery is wrong, for the impact of interpersonal experience it forces one party to suffer, then ANY system of interpretation of other's personal, public & political equality is effectively marginalized or otherwise discriminated against, must be viewed as naturally antithetical to the intent of the 4 words, & their intended social significance.

There can be no arguing with the fact that there was intended to be of a social significance, though maybe all the ways it would manifest, would be beyond the founder's imaginations. Yet, even the inclusion of the process of adding amendments to the Bill of Rights suggests they had some idea that there would be, or already needed to be, a means to establish the reality of an evolving social standard of interpersonal moral concern, thus an evolving social & individual conscience that would need proper means to be established as the law of the land.

This process also to serve as educational, not just proscriptive. For, as we observe in the Civil War, the application of "all are equal" was deemed a debatable issue, even amongst those to whom it never should have been a question.

But that is the history that is Christianity.

Once one imagines that the gods favors oneself over others, then what personal emotional hierarchy of values we hold dearest, will then determine our social actions. For better… or for black America, for worse.

BECAUSE OF THOSE 4 WORDS, SLAVERY COULD BE CONFRONTED, WOMEN RESTORED IN THE RIGHT TO VOTE, ALL HURDLES TO BLACK AMERICA COULD LEGALLY BE REMOVED, IF NOT IN REALITY.

Because of those 4 words, abortion, universal marriage & the abuse of non-Christians could be confronted, if not resolved.

EVERY SOCIALLY EVIL BEHAVIOR MARKETED BY WHITE CHRISTIANS, AS AN ENTITLEMENT GIVEN THEM BY GOD, HAS BEEN EVENTUALLY CONFRONTED BY THOSE 4 WORDS.

But you can't root out of the heart, what wills to be there.

But the Constitution DEMANDS that in time, EVERY IMMORAL OFFENSE PERPETRATED AS SOME RIGHT, WILL BE REVEALED FOR THE FRAUDULENT CLAIM IT IS.

Today, racism, sexists, individuals & corporations who assume a right to use of people & things, are on notice.

Your right to speech, to ANY religious notions you want to entertain, your right to assemble those who agree with you & to communicate in every way, all these 'BEHAVIORS' are secured by the Bill of Rights. That is, providing they do not violate the intent & declared interpersonal social environment it sought to create. An environment, that be it personal, public or political, the ensuing interpersonal relationships will protect & celebrate those four words.

People fail to realize one point: TO HONOR "ALL ARE CREATED EQUAL" IS THE 1ST TIER OF CIVIL OPPORTUNITY & OBLIGATION.

Civil rights, the practice & sharing of civil behaviors, is an opportunity protected for the behavior itself; it is no endorsement, implied or specific, as to the quality of the content of such behaviors. Law & custom imagined to be sufficient to define for the morally impaired the limits of socially allowed behavior.

Hence, once slavery was declared the immoral form of living terrorism it was, then the moral foundations for such exclusionary behavior was also confronted. Yet, because cultural habits had been allowed, knowingly immoral & antithetical to EVERYTHING JESUS TAUGHT WAS A LIFE OF FAITH, then a moral arrogance was continued. A 'right' assumed. A 'right' that nullified the 4 words, not for the effect they should have, but for the denial such people would offer as the measure of their quality of citizenship.

BUT A RIGHT TO A SOCIAL MORALITY NEVER JUSTIFIED NOR LEGITIMIZED BY THE CONSTITUTION OR ANY DOCUMENT ASSOCIATED WITH IT.

Hence, to discriminate against others, in such form as to deny, as in to deny the expression or experience of, or inhibit or limit, the equal experience of the protected & articulated civil rights, is to act against the natural & established interests of the nation, thereby establishing oneself as in an adversarial quality of tension with others, those affected by such anarchy.

Hence, a legitimate question of citizenship & its natural obligations, especially in terms then of the difference between a consumer citizen & a co-creating patriot emerge as social issues. Why?

Because of issues such as racism & sexism.

The use of the freedoms protected by the Bill of Rights, in such moral form as to violate the 1st principle of American citizenship. To accept the reasoned statement that all are created equal, this then offering its own morally significant reality that needs attendance.

This country established a sacred environment, one where the 'unknown' single entity has the moral weight of the whole as its foremost responsibility. Thus, to create a sustainable environment where people of equality can live & flourish, defining a civility that protects that purpose & ensures the public awareness of the movement of history, a movement towards 'beloved community'.

Beloved community the ONLY means to such an ecology of interpersonal values that the environment is stable… civilization exists. Not in numbers of sustained civility, but in a community wherein the relationships are the reason for being, not a coincidence of potential meaning.

When we accept both the wisdom of those four words, as they address both life, living & human need & meaning, as we embrace the potential for maturity, the nature of way we think about our neighbor evolves.

If we have REALLY asked ourselves what kind of politically significant environment do we want to spend our lives in, we must immediately consider the significance of relationships that are implied or demanded.

Hence, we want others to imagine us in the best light, their best light. We desire that they imagine us as equal…

But what are we NOT OWNING?

Relationships of a particular quality are sought… & only those.

Love is the word to describe the relationship held in such a tension of co-created equality & desire for common purpose that all effort is conjoined to that value…

To deny those four words?

To deny the possibility of love to exist.

THAT IS UNCONSTITUTIONAL.

If your values deny me my equality of experience of the Bill of Rights, even you think you offer for God what I need, then you have denied me love & have also denied my opportunity to love.

Please tell me…

WHAT BETTER USE IS THERE TO PUT THE BILL OF
RIGHTS TO THAN TO CO-CREATE BELOVED
COMMUNITY?

WHAT BETTER USE OF THE BEHAVIORS THAN THOSE
THAT WILL THEN PERFECTLY DESCRIBE THE
PATRIOT?

Once you answer these 2 questions… where do YOU fit in?

Why speech, press, religion & association:
The search for wisdom beyond rebellion

(What man hath wrought that is good must be defended...)

"There comes a time when the cup of endurance runs over, & men are no longer willing to be plunged into the abyss of injustice where they experience the blackness of complete despair. I hope, sirs, you can understand our legitimate & unavoidable impatience." M.L. King, Jr.

"...I must confess, that over the last few year, I have been gravely disappointed with the white moderate churches."
M.L. King, Jr.

"The kingdom of God shall be taken from you & given to a nation bringing forth the fruits thereof." Jesus

What should be obvious, now must be stated.

The 'rights' articulated & defended as the 'law of the land', the behaviors to be shared, require a corresponding civility to be realized. That is, if one is honoring the 1st civil right & citizen opportunity to express the ONLY gratitude appropriate to the moment.

'I am free to act' & the proof of that fact is that BOTH of us can share in that behavior, those behaviors, with each other, as a social norm, not the result of a matter of power.

Further, there is even a greater wisdom provided in such a gilded opportunity for community to develop, & of a particular quality.

For, as these men sought to create a sustainable & morally significant foundation for the future of a nation, as to offer respite to the future for what had been denied in the past, in the inclusion of four words, they secured the only value orientation that would not only justify the best humanity has to offer. Further, it would naturally require such interpersonal civility, as a statement of not only our patriotism, but also, more to the point, the final absolute affirmation of our humanity.

'Being human' is now, like in all nature, requiring a morally significant instinct, one to lead us to the maturity needed to be a viable form of life. An instinct that primes us naturally to integrate into a 'social system' & its ecology, with its indicated & needed natural moral nature. We are environmentally mature when we act in such fashion that our living, individually as well as collectively, allows such morally significant community to emerge, that is also environmentally responsible & responsive, that we replicate the very processes of the cosmos in our moral nature.

These founding actors, alone, could never have managed to produce such a quality statement of incorporation & marriage, of such principles & social orientation as they created together.

Hence, they had both a motive & the values necessary & complimentary to need, to secure together what they could not alone. With such morally significant auspicious beginnings, their 1st actions were to embrace an equality of being. Then they could proceed to employ the very behaviors, in civil behaviors, as they would articulate in defense of in the Bill of Rights.

These men then demonstrated, in a time of crisis, the application of the those very behaviors articulated & defended, guided by a moral sense of natural community, to which all people can hale, that then could produce what no one alone could have. The wisdom then of the very values they defended in words, were being justified in behaviors, but behaviors that would illuminate to the world the wisdom of their choices, including four simple words.

These men observed in behavior, in a time of crisis & moral trial, that the ONLY means to community emerges when the values employed are the most inclusive & demand the true heart of integration as it final fruit.

These men were driven by desire & personal agendas as much as any reason to give TO history, what had been denied IN history. But that they employed the principles that can create a sustainable individual, public & political state of community, or a family, offered the insight as to the wisdom that the 'best practices' use of the behaviors protected could yield for a greater whole...

Hence, the witness to the values, the defense of the corresponding needed & human values, was given its greatest authority in the very behaviors of the founders. THEY offered what theory cannot.

A living legacy.

The 'parent' or originating pattern.

If & when we honor, in our hearts, that all ARE created equal, & we deem ourselves not only worthy to the task, but morally & heartistically committed, then we will also be seeking for the fruits of labor that can be shared unilaterally.

As each envisions themselves as their neighbors equal, it is actually a mindset not focused on establishing such social values, it becomes our nature to act in defense of those values, & not merely as an act of honoring law.

When we honor our neighbor as ourselves, it is ourselves we 1st serve. It is ourselves we 1st honor. It is ourselves that we substantially establish as equal to all others.

Why?

Because of the quality of heart behind the offering we will naturally extend as we encounter the opportunity for relationship, be it a moment or a life time.

The heart of love, of caring, naturally seeks such morally significant integration as need, opportunity or desire might offer. When we unilaterally care, then the quality is the same for all, only the circumstances & nature of the offering will vary. This always offering creative opportunity in the 'how' of our choices in caring.

In a pandemic, we wear masks, not as a matter of caving into 'authority', but rather, as a measure of our commitment to that equality, to the need for such community that we can engage the protected civil rights. Our actions, to participate IN community, then is an example of the value of freedom when it is offered to the all. We demonstrate the maturity of accepting that freedom is always a contextual consideration, THAT EVERY CHILD IS TAUGHT FROM INFANCY.

I wear the mask to protect you... from me. Thus, my inconvenience is also then the measure, as your equal, of the value I also place upon myself, you being my 2nd self -image of the citizen/patriot.

With such a celebration of YOUR value, by my wearing a mask, TO PROTECT YOU FROM ANY HARM FROM ME, we become 'beloved community' naturally. For I have done for you no less than I would do for my child. I would do this for you, even you were my enemy. For, to nature & to nature's God, our equality never diminishes the need & moral justification for community... especially, for humanity, beloved community.

Thus, as we wander through life, utilizing such behaviors that were denied so many in history, that are denied yet around the world, we should wonder on the wisdom that ONLY emerges in such community, with such values, realized in committed & sustained behaviors.

Then, we might realize that such behaviors were not just intended for the cavalier or casual, but as the means to realize such wisdom that all can benefit.

As we created in the various amendments that sought to correct what was always morally improper for humanity, to be human, but to which our social conscience as a whole had finally caught up with human experience.

Always a dollar short & a day late... but, wisdom prevailed, even if the child screamed & ranted about loss of freedoms...

Freedoms to harm.

But, the press was NOT meant to be the tool of one personality, one moral viewpoint

Getting it straight: Racism & sexism are neither protected behaviors nor protected rhetoric/speech

(The image of God is 1st observed in others...)

"Who is my mother & who is my brother? He who does the will of my parent... be ye therefore perfect as your parent, loving your enemy that ye be revealed as the children of God..." Jesus

"Did not Moses give you the law; & yet none of you keep the law? Why ye go about to kill me?" Jesus

"You deplore the demonstrations that are presently taking place... But I am sorry that your statement did not express a similar concern for the conditions that brought the demonstrations into being." M. L. King, Jr.

"...Love your enemies & pray for your persecutors; only so that you can be children of your heavenly father..." Jesus
"There must be no limit to your goodness, as your heavenly Father's goodness knows no bounds." Jesus

"Nonviolent direct action seeks to create such a crisis & establish such creative tension that a community that has constantly refused to negotiate is forced to confront the issue. It seeks to dramatize the issue that it can no longer be ignored." M.L. King, Jr.

It was a most disturbing moment. A self-declared white racist asserted, publicly & for the record, that "the Bill of Rights protected his right to hate whomever he chose."

There are so many ways in which that assertion is wrong. Morally wrong, rationally wrong, Constitutionally wrong... nothing really 'right.' Even Jesus is aghast.

What is REALLY critical to grasp is that such a posture, not only is Constitutionally wrong, but is so wrong in that regard as to establish such a posture as to being un-patriotic. It borders upon treason, in the most significant way.

If the 1st morally significant, interpersonally relevant act, as a citizen, is to embrace, recognize & accept the moral authority with which "all... are created equal" was established, then our behavior is the measure of the original commitment to common citizenship 'we' establish, as an act of freedom.

We would stipulate that such a person, in the context of the situation, had acted with maturity... & potentially, wisdom. That depending upon the motives ONLY THAT person truly knows.

The Bill of Rights spells out specific behaviors we are entitled to, as a legal & moral 'right'. BUT... they are a benefit that is to be shared. In as much as there is no innate inequality to morally justify some special entitlement, then, we MUST ASSUME, with authority, that such behaviors are thus to be shared, in common.

If equality of being is the coinage of the realm, then every person under the authority of the founding documents shares in a sacred trust. The freedom to assume for oneself the opportunity to apply our uniqueness, to the needs for community, in such form as to be a potential asset to any interpersonal opportunity.

For if we have TRULY inscribed the words of the Constitution on our heart of hearts, that sacred aspect where ALL we have chosen to care about is held, as treasure, then when we encounter another, it is as if meeting ourselves.

There is no natural basis for discrimination.

Thus, if my assumed biases intruded on either my actions toward you, expressed or otherwise established as recognizable by you, or, if my behavior towards you or in any morally significant proximity limits, hinders, or otherwise unnaturally affects your use of those same protected behaviors, then I have acted against the values & purposes of the nation.

THAT IS NOT A PROTECTED RIGHT.

If the behaviors themselves, that allow & establish some interpersonal discrimination, are a betrayal of America, her values & her people, then even the advancement of such values, as an exercise in speech, religion or any other civil right, cannot be considered civil discourse, much less therefore protected as speech.

American law has finally evolved enough to understand the 'reality' that words creates is the 1st reality, the founding reality. Therefore, there can be such a thing as treasonous rhetoric. Racist rhetoric beyond certain lines is now legally sanctionable. As such, it is un-American.

In that the application of freedom of speech & behavior were not so restricted, that racism in any form was legal, as long as no direct harm could be established, then America, as a nation, created by God, is not possible. A nation created by men, offering the proviso that we honor one another as being equal, this the 1st act of citizenship, cannot long exist under such an assault on its 1st moral premise.

Racism, sexism, both require a devaluing of another, such that we then can morally justify a overt discrimination, of any kind & of any duration, as a natural 'right' of expression. It is the ultimate power play.

It is also the most perfect way to establish 'hate' as the 1st human value.

Just like religiously motivated political behavior, the idea is always about dominating others in such fashion as we ourselves would NEVER consent to suffer.

Further, we must note, for the sake of honest, the arrogance of such postures is beyond the scope of anything that can be morally justified, no matter what god one might try to parade before humanity.

So, from whom are most of the sins of such Americans coming from?

White Christian Americans... & their secular counterparts.

What is needed?

Mothers & fathers who understand the value of the freedoms America offers, the history is took to create this one chance. Then, teach their children the values that then contribute to a patriot state of mind, as opposed to the mere consumer mentality of citizenship so much the norm today. It always being about me & my rights, not our celebration of them as a community.

What is needed?

An enlightened idea of what is real leadership.

Not what is paraded these days, especially by Christians, globally.

What is needed?

A proper understanding of Jesus, his message & mission, that when we offer America is a Christian country, even a Muslim will feel at home... or an atheist.

Barring that? Teach Americans that America has no place for citizen racists & citizens sexists, who will thus terrorize others, with their discriminatory rhetoric & social behaviors. It just ain't the American thing to do... ya know?

It is just treasonous to allow such people to abuse freedom that way... & unloving.

The Alpha Configuration Patriot & Nation:
I defend America's 1st value to the whole
world, starting in my family

(My commitment to you, defines me...)

"ALL... are created equal" Constitution of the US

"Injustice anywhere is a threat to justice everywhere.
Therefore, no American can afford to be apathetic about
the problem of racial injustice. It is a problem that meets
every man at his front door." M.L. King, Jr.

"Let us be dissatisfied. And men will recognize that out of
one blood God made all men to dwell upon the face of the
earth. Let us be dissatisfied until that day when nobody will
shout, "White power!"-when nobody will shout, "Black
power!"..." M.L. King, Jr.

"We, today, need... a means to awaken a sense of shame
within the oppressor & challenge his false sense of
superiority. But the end is reconciliation; the end is
redemption; the end is creation of beloved community... It's
love that will bring about miracles in the heart of men." M.L.
King, Jr.

The greatest honor we can pay a nation, any nation, our own or even our enemy's, is to offer the true quality of civil behavior that naturally honors all its citizens. When we offer a living sense of the absolute values that define the very intended interpersonal nature of relationships, as they develope personally, publicly & politically, then we have offered all we are, all we can be, all we can imagine to be.

When we so honor others, even our enemy, then we have established the true meaning of patriotism.

Patriotism is simply based upon the notion of a 'parent's heart' towards their nation. Parents always assume total responsibility, as a parent. To care about a nation completely, is to have that heart of attendance. Patriots carry forward the values of their nation, that inform their very core of being, as a citizen & family of citizens,

Patriots are the living legacy of a nation's values, superimposed over an entity that has accepted a heartfelt integration of morally significant interpersonal values, as its #1 social effort. All being equal, there is no natural discrimination in our responses to interpersonal opportunity.

As a person in defense of all humanity, that embraces such values that demand such a totality of integration, both as a restorative to history, but also as the ONLY means to the quality of civility sought in history, in the very creation of this nation, to create an alternative & restorative history, the patriot lives the values defended. The patriots as the last standing bastion of its articulation & unique & individual expression. The patriot, in the wisdom of ages, that recognizes & responds to both history & current need, acts as a True Alpha. A 'true' Alpha is one who understands, since humans must & do reason, that reality itself dictates 1st what the terms of occupancy of an environment will be. The Alpha integrates such understanding, thus seeking for the natural wisdom the environment may thus offer naturally.

Since the founding principle of life is established in morally significant sustainable relationships, then wisdom dictates the path forward. To discover a correlative standard of values orientation that can produce, for humanity, the same quality of interpersonal fruits that are sought in any psychologically healthy community. 1st being a morally significant sustainable integration, the critical foundation for community to exist… & develop further.

America provided the foundational value & its logic.

To create community, the best means is to assume an equality of all, justified by all, in the living. With each other. There is no greater means to community & it is the natural derivative rational conclusion that is always experienced in any truly loving family.

Patriotism then, in the context of America, with its defining 1st principle, is to embrace the heart of a parent. Why a parent?

In any community, to sustain its existence, physically much less psychologically as a matter of health & well-being, then the condition of the whole, & its parts, becomes the legitimate concern. A parent, in the training of family, to true family values, recognizes the interpersonal nature of life, & especially as it intersects human life, then assumes a natural role as caretaker, as they had experienced from their parents. Thus, maturity always recognizable in behavior, the standard our families would socialize us to would be to have this interpersonal education so under hand as to be now our 1st nature, not even our 2nd nature.

The patriot, sensitive to the values of the nation, & with that heart, as a parent, trained & socialized since childhood to such human needs for particular values, would naturally extend that heart, learned in the family, valued for the experience if offered. Then, as we master that value orientation, as we processed through the various educational & socializing opportunities we are provided with, we matured in the sense that our social skill, of integration, as a morally significant social agent of great potential effect, we fully committed & thus, we enter into community, mature.

Acting as with the values of a parent, who assumes responsibility for their own living such that in the times of need, they are there. In the quiet times, they are there. The solid citizen is actually a solid patriot.

Citizenship offers one 'products' intended for consumption. These 'commodities' are both mundane but they also include that which gives human life its particular quality of desired & sought meanings. To seek 'to be', not in some abstract sense, but in terms of the moral & social skills needed to not only consume morally, but to offer oneself to a greater creative value, that which is realized ONLY in community, this is our challenge. This is the heart of a parent, who sees within parenting the quality of opportunity for creative offering & creation unparalleled in any other experience.

Thus, as children we merely acted as citizens, ONLY concerned with our own consumption, both physical as well as emotional, emotions the dominant force for any efforts at integration as a child. But, in our socialization, we come to understand, by rote & by experience, the importance of community & thus, the moral means towards integration such that 'beloved community' is its natural creation. It is in choosing how we will 'offer' to others, versus the limits we do or do not place upon our consumption, as a contrast, that defines the patriot then from the 'entitled' citizen.

Thus, as a patriot, as a habit,, such totality of personal investment is then the 'status quo' of offering. It is the 'way of being'. The patriot is an investor, offering what can never be taken, can never be demanded. Acting as a true Alpha, the one who has mastered themselves, in the context of the environment & social & moral ecology they occupy, & then offers the relevant all, contextually, each moment.

Each moment thus merely revealing the 'nature' chosen.

The patriot is never an entity forced to give, to sacrifice. Both speak to what would not be offered, if freedom to choose were an option.

The patriot, in choosing to so care, has removed such limits. The ONLY limits remaining the natural limits of love applied to life.

If my neighbor is equal to my wife, equal to my daughter, then my neighbor is worthy of the same quality of care & social commitment. Thus, in behavior, I actually celebrate such people, by offering them what humanity, in history, denied so many others, continuing such behaviors to this day. Evidence? KKK.

Here then are some of the 'characteristics & a translation of the value 'to care', inspires in the 'patriot'…

A patriot is the 1st line of defense of the most exacting, demanding & morally significant values our nation defines, or even implies.

In this, because of this living witness, such citizens also exhibit all the qualities associated with individual social maturity.

A patriot recognizes the painfilled history of humanity, accepting that the foundation they stand on now, was paid for in blood, sweat & tears; not offered at one time, but spanning generations lost into the fog that is our common history. Hence, even history calls forth a degree & quality of gratitude that then nurtures the natural desire to care we carry within our breasts.

The patriot thus seeks to act as the perfect restorative social agent, bringing into play a standard of social intercourse so as to offer healing to history, by what is now done as the 'way of being'.

Thus, the patriot co-creates such a sacred & secure social environment, that the most vulnerable is as secure as any needed in history.

This means that the patriot offers the world the same hope that the patriot seeks to create here, with others. For America IS the world's people, now concentrated for the final chapter, the final surge to the 'finish line,' when our social maturity is shared universally as more than a vision.

The patriot then is the jealous defender of those 1st principles, offering that if it was good enough for us, it is equally good for the world, hence, the behavioral witness offered by the patriot offers a natural judgment on those leaders, those countries, that refuse to encourage their people to such love, to beloved community.

Accepting "all" are so created, by nature or nature's God, is the act of recognizing the universal natural value of humanity & thus, the values & experiences needed to liberate humanity to its own true potential.

The patriot then defends the sacred value of relationships, as the means for such intercourse between people that all are encouraged to their own 'perfection' & maturity.

The patriot thus is the 1st resource to be offered on the front lines of social experience. They offer to be part of the 'root'; offering to others what they may themselves even be yet incapable of responding to maturely. Hence, even in social confrontation & conflict, the patriot defends the other by defending the value of the developing relationship. Translated, the patriot acts as a true parent would, always committed, even when the going gets tough. The patriot's identity is not rooted in other's feedback, but the original & enduring commitment made to oneself. To love oneself no matter the world we find ourselves in, by remaining true to our human nature, in the need & value of relationships, & thus, sustaining that commitment.

This life lived, is the life of 'faith' that Jesus demanded of those who sought to be children to God. For the atheist or non-theist, that 'faith' in life offered its own witness, its own justification, but creating us. We then 'earn' our place under & with the stars in our heavens.

The patriot thus serves as a source of life, a figure of celebration in its greatest form…continuing the miracle of life… by living it.

The patriot thus, in the witness of values lived, offers all humanity the same witness… as to their own sacred opportunities. Hence, no disheartening discrimination of others between nations is implied or indicated.

Hence, the patriot recognizes the global obligation to offer in all venues possible, the social, political & personal experience of such values. This requires our international relationships embody such commitment.

The patriot seeks for the same benefits for the enemy's children we seek for our own.

This also means, that the 1ˢᵗ & last defense will be the Constitution & its proper morally significant interpretation, as a guide to a living morality, that establishes a sacred community of individuals... iow's... beloved community.

The patriot thus also recognizes the sacred value of 'speech', & honor such behavior by the nature of the guiding moral principles that will be utilized, even with enemy. Always seeking to secure sacred opportunity for relationship, as the ONLY means to confront evil & encourage restoration & repentance. These are the peace makers Jesus spoke to.

This kind of critical consciousness, that creates a sustainable community-mind set, is no less the very principles lived & offered in the family. Hence, the tradition of family, its true family values given life.

This investment offers that the patriot is a form of living social conscience. Always affirming the value of the individual, in a vector of constantly changing relationships.

The patriot is thus the guiding national figure whose very being is defined by the 1ˢᵗ & most compelling flagship value of America... that truly, ALL ARE EQUAL, BUT ONLY REALIZED IN THE LIVING WITNESS WE OFFER, 1ˢᵀ, TO EACH OTHER.

Who then is a family member, of America?

ANY who live by such values, who offer such values, are a true patriot, even their own nation not as yet embracing such universally needed & demanded values.

UNIVERSAL PATRIOTISM IS CREATED ANEW EACH DAY... IN THE HEARTS & BEHAVIORS OF MILLIONS, ONLY YET TO RECOGNIZE ONE ANOTHER.

That is the challenge & hope America offers her citizens... or the world.

Would that Americans so acted as patriots, rather than immature children not to be trusted with big child toys. Like freedom.

The 3 Great Human Virtues in the Time of the Global Patriot: For whom the bell tolls...

(Owning & propagating our 'humanity')

"...we will take direct action against the injustice without waiting for other agencies to act. We will not obey unjust laws or submit to unjust practices. We will do this peacefully, openly, & with nonviolence because our end is a community at peace with itself. Martin L. King, Jr.

"Men, for years now, have been talking about war & peace. But now, no longer, can they just talk about it. It is no longer a choice between violence & nonviolence in this world; it's nonviolence or nonexistence." Martin L. King, Jr.

"You do not do evil to those who do evil to you, but you deal with them with forgiveness & kindness." Prophet Mohammad

"... be ye therefore perfect, loving your enemy, that the true children of God might be revealed..." Jesus

  After several hundred years of oppression, slavery, & every imaginable & unimaginable degradation, humiliation & physical & psychological form of possible harm, Black America is once again pleading, "when is enough, ENOUGH?"

  Unfortunately, because of the personal, day to day living experience of that, forced even into the home, in the pathologies such suffering forces upon people, Black America dares not equally seek to understand the dark well of history that reveals theirs is merely a song that has yet to find a proper ending.

When I look into my soul, a soul that that is the fruit of thousands of years of social evolution, I observe a tortured soul, a being seeking a 'home', a home defined by the nature of community.

Some will nod their heads, imagining their wisdom to place my focus solely on my family history of deprivation. There is no doubt such experiences were 'priming' experiences, creating significant deficient. But then, if that be true, my seeking healing is a good sign, better than most who have suffered such PTSD quality of life experiences.

The adult crushed by life experiences, that cannot be heartistically & rationally processed, finding ourselves bereft the skills & values that we thought we had access to, that would at least act as a buffer; then we despair & lose hope, imagining ourselves alone in such a way that others cannot fathom, & from a place we cannot reach out of.

As a child, I knew no disappointment to entertain, as such experiences force on one. I had no such correlative referential point. A child cannot have expectations in the sense most imagine as adults. Our hell is a totality with meaning, but one we cannot grasp, even for the evil it may reveal. Thus, as a child, completely vulnerable in a different way, but no less profound for the impact.

Yet, as I entered & have occupied the world, that upon encountering me, others assume a greater 'health' psychologically, yet seem to participate in this world willingly, with no real desire for any change. Apathetically satisfied with their ½ acre & late model car, in lieu of the traditional mule.

But whether PTSD is experienced as a vulnerable child, or as a vulnerable human being, it all cycles back to one issue; the values that humanity continues to employ, with impunity, imagined as some 'right', merely because to date, it can be 'forced' upon humanity.

With the creation of America, history had a 2nd shot to correct the failure of humanity 2000 years earlier, when the 1st

clear opportunity for a final morally significant social evolution occurred, centering on the Jewish people, & certain social actors in its history.

As we have explored the universal & cosmic significance of interpersonal relationships, to life & living, we cannot ignore, with any moral authority, the social value of the standard Jesus sought to establish, as the human norm. The demands of life, of human life, of living, all dictate their own ecological moral system, that must be employed, to justify the human, as a species that will continue to exist.

We stand at a precipice the likes of which we have never encountered previously.

It is either create… or extinction.

Jesus established, in his words, that 3 related social values & subsequent behaviors were the final key to human freedom &… happiness.

As previously offered, the 1st condition of a parent, of a patriot, is the posture of a quality of ownership, that while not possessing, nor offering any tangible asset other than the self, offers an all, to all.

Life being what it is & childhood a process of socializing experiences, to nurture the development of a 'human', being human, then the application of such a standard of common commitment, as we imagine love to truly be, it is then challenged as to the needed form & any correlative emotional content.

The most common form altering challenge love naturally encounters is two forms of deviance from children. The initial form of deviance from children is encountered in the process of discovering the universe is a varying but stable set of relationships, demanding various kinds & qualities of responses. The 1st challenge is that we must share this universe. Thus, as a child 'acts', with socially informing consequences, the demands of love will vary. The most common is the need to re-educate about some aspect of intercourse that was anti-social or at least, negative in its impact. Hence, forgiveness may be needed, the forgiveness that is in such relationship that a personal attendance is natural & required, to re-establish such quality of relationship, that any harm is immediately sought to be restored, as opportunity & willingness from the child will allow.

Even children must master some form of degree of this social skill, for every relationship will pose the possibility of interpersonal harm, & if our commitment, in part or toto is sufficient, we will then want to remain as an asset to the other &/or the relationship. Hence, even self-interest can be rationally defended, if it serves a greater purpose. To forgive frees one from the past, to act in the present, as an aid to a future.

The application of commitment to 'care', the font & foundation for love to emerge, is thus a resource suitable to many situations, even deviance. Thus, this most significant of forms of love is the 2nd most important interpersonal social value & orientation sufficient both to potential & human need.

Once we deviate, we have in some form, created a harm, or a potential for harm, to be 'normalized' into human experience. If the socialization of a child were complete, then we naturally would seek to restore ourselves as we matured, socialized to the value of community & our place in it & as a co-creator of it. But even in this world, people understand the value of repentance… as a means to restore stability in a relationship offended by deviance & as a means to re-establish community.

When we understand the real nature of repentance, we quickly grasp the fact that as love goes, repentance is also to act with love, thus, it too is an act of creation.

We discover that repentance is thus also a celebration of life & living, even if of a restorative nature. The effect is beloved community. It is a self-correcting mechanism that is focused on restoring then potential value of the original relationship. It is perfect use of human will, offers no loss of freedom, of any kind or quality.

Together, these 3 forms of commitment to otherness beyond self-interest, create The 3 Great Human Virtues that define the ONLY values needed for human consumption, to define the human, being, as a human being.

If the true patriot of America defends, in their living, the values of America, to integrate into such sustainable community that all citizens can equally share in the experience of protected behaviors the Constitution demands for all of us, then such a person naturally will act as a global patriot.

For if "ALL" share in being such a creation, then ALL places such a designation not ONLY on Americans sharing, since the ONLY true Americans would then be the indigenous peoples. Any descendants of immigrants, after the settlement of the original natives, would thus also qualify as an alien.

A Personal Letter to 'white' Christian Americans from Jesus

(A few choice words also offered by Paul & others)

"Why call me Lord, Lord, & not do the things I say? Love your enemy, that ye be known as the true children of God…

WHOM IS MY MOTHER & BROTHER? Why must I remind you to this day? Do you REALLY care so little for your heavenly parent that you refuse to abide by my words?

Well hath Alia prophesied of you hypocrites. As it is written, this people draweth nigh onto me with their mouth; this people adoreth me with their lips; but their heart is far from me. How be it in vain do they worship me…

They have forgotten or choose to ignore that I have offered that not everyone that saith unto me, Lord, Lord, shall enter into the kingdom of heaven; but he that doeth the will of my father. Hence, to become perfect as my father in heaven.

Did not Moses give you the law & yet, none of you keepth the law? What is the greatest commandment? To love God with all your heart, your mind & your soul! The 2nd is like the 1st…. to love your neighbor as yourself!

Yet no church today teaches such a standard of filial piety. Why? Did you, do you think I jest? Do not assume to be safe… even Satan acknowledges the son before the parent… you must do much more…

Is that the social reality I observe in America, from whites claiming to be 'Christian'? I did not come to abolish the law, but to fulfill it… But I know you… that ye have not the love of God in you. Unless you show yourselves far better than the religious leaders surrounding & misleading you, you can never enter the coming kingdom…

Hence, LOVE YOUR ENEMIES... THAT YE BE KNOWN AS THE CHILDREN OF YOUR FATHER!

There must be no limit to your goodness, as your heavenly father's goodness knows no limits. Pray quickly, repenting that the wrongful you have done can be forgiven, as you venture forth to forgive others you have instead engaged as enemies.

I have warned you... if you have love only for those who love you, what reward can you expect from heaven, what recognition? Drug addicts, politicians & criminals do as much as that! Hence, if you do not forgive & love others, what demands can you place before your heavenly father?

Why then call me Lord, Lord, & not doeth that which I say? No one can serve two masters; for either he will hate the 1st & love the 2nd, or he will be devoted to the 1st & despise the 2nd. You cannot serve God & mammon.

How little faith you exhibit to the world! How much you deny me & my father... who seeks to serve you as any parent attends their children, no matter how deviated from family values. Do not ask anxiously, 'What will we eat? What will we drink?' These are the things that occupy the minds of the heathen, politician, capitalist; but your heavenly father knows you need them all. Rather, set your mind on God's kingdom & God's justice before ANYTHING else...

ALWAYS treat others as you would like them to treat you; that is the law & the prophets... & not one word, not one jot of the law will pass away until ALL is fulfilled... be ye therefore perfect as your heavenly parent, that ye be KNOWN as the children of that parent.

Do not store up for yourselves treasure on the earth, where moth & rust destroy & thieves break in & steal; but store up treasures in heaven... for where your treasures are, there will be your heart also.

You have forgotten... I came not to bring peace...but a sword. I have come to set a man against his father, a daughter against her mother... & a man will find enemies under his own roof... NO ONE IS WORTHY OF ME WHO LOVES FATHER OR MOTHER MORE THAN ME...

Who then is MY mother & brothers & sisters? They are those who do the will of our heavenly parent, becoming perfect even in the love offered to one's enemy, never forgetting we each were the enemy of God, but for God reaching out to us... Therefore, express the ONLY gratitude worthy of the word... behavior!

Blessed are those who do not find me an obstacle to faith... ever since the time of John the Baptist, the kingdom of heaven has been & is being subjected to violence & violent men are taking if by force even now! Look to your halls of government, the centers where God even seeks to affect the business of humanity... yet, how can I describe this generation?

You brood of vipers!

Alas for you, America! Alas for you who falsely claim to be Christian. If the miracles performed in the past you hold as faith had happened in Sodom & Gomorrah, they would have repented long ago in sack cloth & ashes! Yet you parade a president before me who mocks every value your heavenly parent lives by & teaches you to live by! This is your gratitude?

What will happen to you white Christians in your mockery? Will you be exalted to heaven? NO! You will be brought now to Hades! Do you think that mere years would wear down the standard of heaven, to unite with the heathen & anarchist? Repent!

EVERY kingdom divided against itself is laid waste... look around you. He who is not with me, to do as our heavenly parent wills, is thus against me! He who does not gather with me, scatters & offers to evil. Therefore, BE AS MATURE IN YOUR LOVE AS YOUR PARENT, THUS GIVING WITNESS AS TO YOUR TRUE LINEAGE...

BUT BE WARNED! Every thoughtless word you speak you will have to account for on the Day of Judgment. For out of your own mouth you will be judged; out of your own mouth you will be condemned.

Did you think my death altered the meaning of one word I uttered? Is not the God of the Jews your God also? Then why think that what I spoke to them in the authority of our parent is not also held to be your own portion?

Who is MY mother? Who are my brothers? Whomever does the will of my heavenly parent... love your enemy that ye be known as the children of YOUR parent.

Was it not good seed that you sowed in your fields? So where have all the evil weeds come from? Why the racism? Why the sexism? Why the abuse of the creation? Is this your gratitude?

Did you create the resources of your nation? Are YOU the authors of creation? Do you understand the meaning of stewardship? Is America a nation that honors the creation? Do ALL her children experience the same joy of living, of sustained community, the fruits of the resources inherited, by no other effort than being born? Or are they siphoned off & controlled by the least worthy?

LISTEN! UNDERSTAND1 No one is defiled by what goes into his mouth; ONLY by what comes out of it. OR ARE YOU AS DULL AS THE REST? What comes out of the mouth has its origin in the heart, that which is the source of the sacred values we hold as our deepest treasures... hence, that is what defiles a person. Wicked thoughts, murder, ADULTARY, FORNICATION, THEFT, PERJURY, SLANDER... ALL THESE PROCEED FROM THE HEART...

Therefore, MUST I KEEP REMINDING YOU? REPENT... LOVE... EVEN TO YOUR ENEMY... USE YOUR WORDS ONLY TO SERVE...

To those who seek the reins of power... they are NOT an entitlement... TO SERVE is a blessing & sacred opportunity. Hence, whomever exalts himself will be humbled... the greatest among you must be your servant... SO TOO IT MUST BE AMONG NATIONS!

Alas for you, Christian hypocrite! You shut the door to the kingdom of heaven in people's faces... globally... in the witness to your hate of others & self-entitlements! Hence, you do not enter the kingdom yourselves & when others try to enter, you stop them.

Alas for you, Christian hypocrite! You travel over sea & land to win one convert; & when you have succeeded, you make him twice as fit for hell as you are yourselves... REPENT!

Alas for you, blind guides, hypocrites! You pay tithes of coin & paper; but you have overlooked the weightier demands of the law... JUSTICE, MERCY, & GOOD FAITH... IT IS THESE YOU SHOULD HAVE PRACTICED!

Alas you Christian hypocrite! You are like tombs covered with whitewash; they LOOK fine on the outside, but inside they are full of dead men's bones & corruption. So it is with you... inside you are full of hypocrisy & lawlessness. Have you no shame?

Oh, America, America! City on the Hill... that murders the children of slaves torn from their homes to this day... from their home shores. These children your Heavenly Parent loves no less than yourselves... or your children; it is their LIVING forgiveness that has stayed my hand from moving against you!

How often would I have gathered your children to me, as a hen gathers her brood under her wings... but you would not let me embrace ALL your children! Look at America now! Divided, forsaken & laid waste! I tell you; you will not see me until the time when you say, with all your heart, "Blessed are ALL the children of the Lord!"

Many false prophets have risen... they occupy every church; every crevice evil can squeeze into or through. They are misleading most... the 'true' love of many never matured or has grown cold...

The gospel is YET to be fully revealed throughout the world... then the end will come. Do NOT look for a sign... the sign of Jonah is your portion... for a wicked generation mocks heaven, in the witness it now offers the world...

YOU ARE NOT READY FOR THE BRIDEGROOM... WHAT GIFTS HAVE YOU TO OFFER?

What enemy joins you to honor the one who gave YOU skin touch with God?

Teaching them to observe all I have commanded of you?

Be ye therefore perfect as your heavenly parent...

Repent America! Repent white 'Christian'... or suffer the fate of those who mock heaven & assume mere belief is passage to heaven...

The world hateth me… because I testify of it… that the works there are evil… not everyone that saith unto me, 'Lord, Lord', shall enter the kingdom of heaven… BUT HE THAT DOETH THE WILL OF MY PARENT…

A Letter from Paul, et al…

When we observe the state of American Christianity as embraced & offered, especially by the self-designating white community… well…

They have become filled with every kind of wickedness, evil, greed & depravity. They are full of envy, murder, strife, deceit & malice. Their leaders model this behavior as the 'rights of man'. They are gossips, slanderers, insolent, arrogant & boastful; they invent ways of doing evil, led by a man who lied 18,000 times in 3 years of employment. They have no understanding of their evil, no fidelity, no love, no mercy. Although they know God's righteous decree, that those who do such things deserve DEATH, they not only continue to do these very things but also approve of those who practice them.

It is past time to repent…

… it is not those who hear the law, who offer a rhetorical witness to Jesus who will be saved & are righteous in God's sight… BUT IT IS THOSE WHO OBEY THE LAW WHO WILL BE DECLARED RIGHTEOUS…

But because of your stubbornness & your unrepentant heart, you are storing up wrath against yourself for the day of God's wrath…God will repay each person for what they have done…

What shall we conclude then?

There is no one righteous, not even one; there is no one who understands; there is no one who seeks God in righteous behavior. All have turned away, they have together become worthless; there is not one of them that does good, not even one. Their throats are open graves; their tongues practice deceit. The poison of vipers is on their lips. Their mouths are full of cursing & bitterness. Their feet are swift to shed blood, to shame & isolate the true heart, ruin & misery mark their ways, & the way of peace they do not know. THERE IS NO FEAR OF GOD BEFORE THEIR EYES...

Those who live according to the flesh, have their minds set on what the flesh desires... The mind governed by the flesh is death... the mind governed by the flesh is hostile to God. Those who are in the realm of the flesh CANNOT please God.

Love must be sincere... niceness is not love. Hate what is evil...Honor one another above yourselves... Do NOT be proud... be willing to associate with people of low position, they the children of heaven no less than oneself. Do not repay evil with evil.

IF YOUR ENEMY IS HUNGRY, FEED HIM... IF HE IS THIRSTY, GIVE HIM DRINK...

Do not be like your POTUS... Give to everyone what you owe them... Let no debt remain outstanding... instead, love others as you have been loved.

The time has already come for you to wake up from your slumber... because our universal salvation is nearer now than when we 1st began our spiritual paths. So, let us put aside the deeds of darkness... Let us behave decently... not in sexual immorality, not in dissension & jealousy... do not think about how to satisfy the desires of the flesh.

You MUST NOT ASSOCIATE WITH ANYONE WHO IS SEXUALLY IMMORAL OR GREEDY!! Do not associate with a slanderer or swindler. Neither the SEXUALLY IMMORAL, the ADULTERERS, NOR THIEVES NOR THE GREEDY WILL INHERIT THE KINGDOM OF GOD!

REPENT, AMERICA!

Flee from sexual immorality... All other sins a person commits are outside the body, but whomever sins sexually sins against their own body.

Love is patient... love is kind. It does not boast, it is not proud. It does not dishonor others. It is not self-seeking. It is not easily angered. Love rejoices with the truth. LOVE NEVER FAILS...

DO NOT BE MISLED; BAD COMPANY CORRUPTS GOOD CHARACTER... Do not be led by such people, they will lead you to hell...

Put to death, therefore, whatever belongs to your earthly nature; sexual immorality, impurity, evil desires & greed... Because of these... the WRATH OF GOD IS COMING.

DO NOT LET ANYONE DECEIVE YOU IN ANY WAY... LEST YOU FOLLOW THE MAN OF LAWLESSNESS, THE MAN DOOMED TO DESTRUCTION. He will oppose & will exalt himself over all others... seeking to be worshipped & thus, sets himself up as God's 'temple' for the people to gather around... proclaiming himself to be equal to God... by the nature of the unprincipled behaviors he will claim is his right to impose on others, whom he considers either enemies or pawns to be manipulated.

Whomever seeks to be an overseer, a manager of people & resources that belong to the community, he must be above reproach, faithful to his wife, temperate, self-controlled, respectable, hospitable, not violent but gentle... NOT A LOVER OF MONEY!!!!

Treat younger men as brothers, older women as mothers, & YOUNGER WOMEN AS SISTERS, WITH ABSOLUTE PURITY.

Those elders who are sinning you are to reprove before everyone, so that others may take warning. COMMAND those who are rich in this world to not be arrogant... not to put their hope in wealth. COMMAND them to do good, to be rich in good deeds & to be generous & willing to share.

Warn a divisive person once & then warn them a 2nd time. AFTER THAT HAVE NOTHING TO DO WITH THEM... You may be sure that such people are warped & self-centered; THEY ARE SELF-CONDEMNED.

Marriage should be honored by all & the marriage kept pure, for God will judge the adulterer & all the sexually impure... Keep your lives free of the love of money.

Do not merely listen to the word... DO WHAT IT SAYS.

Now, listen, you rich people, weep & wail because of the misery that is coming on you. Your wealth has rotted... your gold & silver are corrupted; their corrosion will testify against you & eat your flesh... You have hoarded wealth & the wages you failed to pay the workers are crying out against you… Their cries have reached the ears of the almighty Lord.

America was a land blessed… but not for the people living there alone. God blessed America that it might be a blessing onto the world, as a good witness to the truth of God & the truth of the universal God nurtures for ALL the children of the earth…

Hence, REPENT AMERICA… OR FACE GOD'S WRATH… YOUR FAITH IS ONLY ASHES… YOUR HEART IS DEAD… AMERICA, & THE WORLD, SUFFERS FOR YOUR ARROGANCE.

REPENT, OR THE FRUITS OFFERED YOU WILL BE TAKEN & OFFERED TO A NATION THAT WILL ACT WITH GOD, NOT AGAINST GOD…

YOU HAVE BEEN WARNED…

(Only lightly paraphrased or with some addition, the content offered is directly from the New Testament… people assuming that they are saved MERELY on the foundation of some declaration of filial piety… if hell exists, created by humanity or God… most of Christianity in America is in for a most rude experience… & will blame everyone else except who is truly culpable…the man in the mirror.)

Book 5

Movement towards global righteousness

The Trump/American Hoax: Socialism as communism & un-American & other children's stories to terrify & divide

(Fear & ignorance ARE NOT BLISS)

"The way of violence leads to a bitterness in the survivors & brutality in the destroyers. But, the way of nonviolence leads to redemption & the creation of beloved community."
Martin L King, Jr

"The established religions & their adherents have never realized that man has a central responsibility for turning this evil world around." Rev. Sun Myung Moon

"If freedom is to be extended, it must discipline itself both personally & communally. On the personal level this means developing a unity of purpose so that choosing & action are harmonious for the self. This also involves a communal awareness & concern for the individual is part of society. Thus, unity has normative features in conjunction with freedom." John K Roth

"Because human beings are created to live in an ideal society, they will inevitably pursue a socialistic ideal as they strive for freedom & democracy & further search into their original nature... As this natural desire springs forth from within, politics in democracy, which is shaped by the will of the people, will move in that direction. EVENTUALLY, A SOCIALISTIC SOCIETY EMBODYING GOD'S IDEAL WILL BE ESTABLISHED... "Responding to the promptings of their innermost hearts, people everywhere have ardently aspired to the world of God's ideal... In seeking for a socialist society on heaven's side, their original mind has drawn them to the ideals of interdependence, mutual prosperity & universally shared values. The world in which these ideals will finally be realized is none other than the Kingdom of Heaven on earth..." Rev. Sun Myung Moon & The Exposition of the Divine Principle

The greatest threat to global peace as an 'external threat' DOES ORGINATE IN COMMUNIST STATES & THIS THREAT MUST BE VIEWED WITH EVERY DEGREE OF SERIOUSNESS & MATURITY WE CAN MUSTER AS CITIZENS & AS PATRIOTS. But we need a reasoned & informed populace, not emotionally immature driven bigots throwing rhetoric & sounds bytes around as if truly engaging & properly interpreting reality.

It is a time to seek wisdom.

But, there is a greater threat to global peace & prosperity... it is the world impact of a Trump led, Christian morally dominated nation, confronting China & Russia.

China & Russia MUST act as expansionists because the essence of their ideology is a 'messianic call' more compelling than Christianity's siren response to the idea of a 2nd coming of Jesus. China is laying claim to Asia except for the Middle East. Russia is staking out South & Central America, where racism against Asians is harder to overcome. But they both seem able to work in Africa, the need so great, racism a fact of life. In the

US, conservative elements would seek complete moral control of what civil rights we will have, to what degree & in what form.

This ultimately means that Christians are seeking a control of the nation that will forever change its essential value orientation. "All... are created equal' will cease to exist as the national anthem for integration & community. Rather, the 'chosen' among the created will assume a stewardship over the population in certain areas of moral concern to them, in the form it offends them.

In America, neither the right nor the left appear properly motivated to distinguish either the nature of the threats we do face, internally & externally, much less offer the vision & values needed to garner the informed decisions we need to make. Such values then illuminating the adjustments required, both in our own way of responding as individuals & families & the social response internally & externally Americans need to reconsider as national & global priorities.

But...

There are few things that irritate me quite as much as the wholesale bull shit rhetoric used against both socialism & liberalism. During my most rabid & most intolerant existence as a political entity, as a Republican, I was want to imagine all things liberal as also deviant, anti-American, unchristian & encompassing any other values as to render liberals as 'less' American. Hence, less human. But... to confuse matters for me, I also discovered that Democrats were not single minded in their avoidance of hard truth.

Rather, during that same period I also held that the Democrats, EXCEPT FOR ANY TOTALITARIANS WHO SEEK TO DESTROY THE ENEMY, RATHER THAN INTEGRATE WITH THEM, that the party actually sought to protect the 'heart' of America. The 'caring' about people that requires we offer no less than we take as our measure. The Democrats were the heart that remembered, that in the end, it IS all about the people.

As a Republican, I had imagined that we were also about principles & protecting resources, for the sake of the future. As a lecturer in a program called Victory Over Communism, we grasped the error of Marxism & other such forms of ultimate political expedience, hiding the real intended ideological revenge sought against ANY resisting humanity. In response we sought to educate a reluctant & uncaring populace. To no avail.

The result of American Christian willful ignorance? A staggering 200 million dead in less than a century.

But don't go waving any flags in protest.... that number ONLY exists BECAUSE OF THE FAILURE OF CHRISTIANITY IN HISTORY TO BOTH PROTECT & TO DISSEMINATE THE TRUE & FULL MESSAGE OF JESUS.

We know the rhetoric...Communism was a problem over there... except for the commies in our midst. Which have become the foil for any kind & quality of attack to be thrust at all liberals & Democrats.

Hence, in the failure of Christianity to champion the true & full message of Jesus, Christianity became an institution more interested in its own moral & physical solvency & political power than in acting as champions for Jesus. In this failure then, Marx was justified for the judgement of Christianity & capitalism, but completely failed when that judgement led to the desire to destroy that which he felt could not be changed.

Where a righteous judgement as to the evils of a system of deciding human value that allowed various forms of slavery to exist was, & is still needed, given the essence of the values that would define capitalism by Marx's time, through church & governments, in the dominating of others for the sake of personal & political profit & power, Marx & others allowed their righteous anger to become a consuming desire for change. But that the search for the BEST MORAL MEANS TO PERSUASION WERE SET ASIDE FOR THE MORE EMOTIONALLY SATISFYING, IF PROFOUNDLY IMMATURE RESPONSE OF THE ANGRY, RESENTFUL & VENGEFUL CHILD? AN ADULT CHILD NOT YET TRULY SOCIALIZED TO THE ABSOLUTE HUMAN NECCESSITY FOR MORALLY SIGNIFICANT, HUMAN WILLED SUSTAINABLE RELATIONSHIPS? THE QUALITY NEEDED TO LIVE & OFFER THE QUALITY OF PERSONAL, PUBLIC & POLITICAL MEANING ALL HUMANS NATURALLY SEEK?

Then we have Marxism, Maoism...we have the ultimate form of justice... a justice that destroys the enemy or so subjugates them as to create a sustainable form of slavery.

A slavery that demands little, because it has little to offer. Because the desire is not for universal suffrage… it is for control of others, such that resistance & rebellion do not exist in any socially significant way.

THIS IS NOW THE SOCIAL, RELIGIOUS & POLITICAL AGENDA OF THE CONSERVATIVE CHRISTIAN MOVEMENT IN AMERICA.

Christian America is now the new form of atheism. For the founder is nowhere to be discovered in word, deed or intent of the conservative Republican Christian. Neither in rhetoric offered as political discourse nor in church spiritual interpretations & prophesy.

Christian prophesy now serves anti-American values… anti-Jesus values. Hence, offering a vision of America, the president, the country & its future 100% at odds with Jesus… & therefore, we must assume, God.

Hence, even though Rev. Moon himself called for an integration of religion with government, it was absolutely & ONLY focused on the values that Jesus demanded a true child of God would naturally manifest, as their 'acts of faith'. This requires that EACH CITIZEN WOULD THEN ACT AS THE FRONT LINE DEFENSE OF THE VALUES THAT ARE INTEGRATED INTO THE SOCIAL ENVIRONMENT, BOTH AS PERSONAL & PUBLIC DISCOURSE & AS BEHAVIOR.

In other words, the national norm would reveal a quality of natural civility that offered a perfect witness to the social reality that "all… are created equal" & the public witness is that evidence. THIS IS THE ONLY STANDARD OF INTEGRATION OF RELIGION & GOVERNMENT THAT CAN BE MORALLY JUSTIFIED FOR ANY CULTURE.

RELIGION ALONE IS NO JUSTIFICATION TO DOMINATE THE GREATER CULTRUE…NOT IN A WORLD OF THEISTS.

At one time, the kind of 'heart' that also protects America, for her values, such as "ALL… are created equal," ALSO was part of the values imagined to be defended by Republicans.

When I now observe the willingness to destroy the environment, for the sake of profit, political leverage, status & power, I KNOW the Republican Party neither serves the nation, her principles, & sadly, for the reputation we tried to sell like snake oil, neither Jesus nor God… well, any one's god except self-interest. I observe a people so baffled by life that they have allowed unprincipled minds & access to unearned wealth to 'buy' laws created only to serve a slave master's mindset & to be used to 'hustle' the people out of every farthing they can… or dollar.

When we rationally understand the 'demanded' values that define the very nature that separates this nation from most others, in the inclusion of a moral foundation that requires the very principles of civility & community that establishes & defines a life of faith & gratitude, we realize the covenant & trust history has bequeathed us, merely for being born here & in this time.

Hence, the greater moral obligation to a quality of human maturity that creates & honors the ONLY path to human maturity… & thus true love community, would bear all the earmarks of a living & lived gratitude.

One that confronts the essence of Marxism, capitalism, racism, sexism, environmental atheism & other such unprincipled & hence, truly godless ideological rationales. To honor America's values is to offer the perfect criticism of communism… & unprincipled Christianity.

The Christianity of Trump is the communism of the right wing, seeking NOT God's kingdom, but a new form of godless hell. Just worse than they one they are trying to orchestrate now.

A Christian minister who nationally declares that inter-racial marriages are Satan's means to destroy America & is celebrated & supported by communists as the means to help destroy America, then I KNOW God is not on the pulpit in America.

When white America is silent… when such heart dominates the words of the leaders, then the people cannot be far behind. Or they would not be in attendance & their rebellion would be heard & celebrated in heaven.

Yet, as I listen to the televangelists, I hear the most horrible of teachings, the most imaginative material to deceive & distract.

I must admit, stories of alien abductions strike me as more credible. I don't expect aliens… unless it is us returning to the earth in the future.

Socialism can take at least two forms.

One form is the communist form. It is inherently evil. It seeks to destroy what it cannot persuade or convert. It seeks to dominate, at any cost. Except to itself.

The other is what I call a principled socialism.

The 1st principle defines all the others.

:All… are created equal."

Then we work to define how to sustain THAT personal, public & political reality… Hint.

We incorporate the words used to define a human… being Jewish. Or American.

Love God with all your being. No BS this time. Love your neighbor as yourself, no less. Never leave an enemy behind, he is still family.

THAT IS TRUE SOCIALISM.

This is what Trump, his kind & the Christian right CANNOT do.

Then where are our patriots?

Not in the Republican Party or its media support system.

But repentance is always the way home.

Hence, always hope… always hope.

But the rest of us must never waver… socialism is NOT communism. Socialists, true socialists, are 1st & foremost natural environmentalists. For we observe the natural & healthy environment, we understand its moral ecological system… & we integrate.

Heart, mind, soul… & all our resources. Because we have chosen to care THAT much.

That is NOT capitalism.

That is NOT America… yet.

That is NOT communism.

Bended knees, raised fists & the true patriot in the times of trouble: Remembering the righteous rebels King, Gandhi & Camus

('I' protest that 'we' become beloved community)

"The question is, "Did you, as the owner, do all you could to save this nation?" Rev. S.M. Moon

"First & foremost morality is about defining the parameters of moral significance to relationships, thus mitigating, educating & directing the social conscience, seeking to enhance the impact of freedom on & in relationships by behavior. It is about addressing the anti-social motives & resulting behaviors that impact the social environment. Hence, the 1st freedom & most critical value to be considered will be the use of our reasoning to engage the consideration of my neighbor as if myself." Chris Jordan

"If all mankind minus one, were of one opinion, & only one person of the contrary opinion, mankind would be no more justified in silencing that one person, than he, if he had the power, would be justified in silencing mankind... If the opinion is right, they are deprived of the opportunity of exchanging error for truth; if wrong, they lose, what is almost as great a benefit, the clearer perception & livelier impression of truth, produced by its collision with error." John Stewart Mill

"...if we are to speed up the coming of the new age, we must have the moral courage to stand up & protest against injustice wherever we find it... I realize this will mean suffering... It might even mean physical death." M.L. King, Jr.

"I never intend to adjust myself to mob rule. I never intend to adjust myself to the tragic effects of the methods of physical violence ..." M.L. King, Jr.

"God grant we will be so maladjusted that that we will be able to go out & change our world & our civilization." M.L. King, Jr.

"No longer will the rhetoric of hate & marginalization dominate... It is the time to honor relationships for the value to life they are, as the ONLY means to create & sustain life. If you won't love, then please repent. There is no room in the world for people who continue to choose not to commit. Commit or be committed. You will not get away with not loving... because a world is coming that to not love will hurt everyday... will crush your spirit. Either you learn to love, to repent, to forgive, or expect to go the way of the Dodo... a well-earned EXTINCTION! The world will not long suffer you & your arrogance. Repent, or expect to be loved to death! Such is the justice of heaven... or earth! This is no Sunday School emotionalism... this is the love that takes it to the enemy & baby.... here we come!" Posted on Facebook, with permission

One of America's more shameful moments, actually among hundreds, was when a young black American took to his knee, this during the playing of the national anthem.

It was NOT HIS ACTIONS that were disgraceful & shameful.

It was when someone call him a 'son of a bitch'.

A man who dared suggest that social protest against systemic racism in America, that flourishes to this day, rather, was an attack against the nation, its flag & veterans.

By a man who refused service himself, not once, but 3 times, using money & position to manipulate the system, a pattern he would perfect over the next decades.

A man who disgraced a sacred trust & the power of the position he occupies, by using that position to seek to malign another's life... & therefore livelihood, based upon his own racism.

When we deny reality, for those with no power or limited or limited access to power, then the recourse needed for social confrontation of a healthy nature, is just not there. How to force such issues to be taken seriously is a question of ethical persuasion with no simple answers.

Immediately we realize we have reached a point of no return.

How to rebel.

Even as enemies, arm in arm, we integrate: The social legacies of Sun Myung Moon & Jesus

(I forgive that 'WE' might be...Love entertaining no consciousness of self...)

"But the end is reconciliation; the end is redemption; the end is the creation of the beloved community." Martin L. King, Jr.

"The maxim of philosopher's concerning the conditions under which the public peace is possible shall be consulted by nations armed for war." Emmanuel Kant

"It is never proper to seek 'to be good'; equally, it is never proper to seek 'to do good'. Neither are the aspirations to love, to be part of community. The 'fruit of being' produced in living should be good, but it is not the purpose of being to seek for these 'results'. They are the natural products of a 'way of being.' Hence, we do not 'earn' our value as social agents when we seek to create 'good', rather our value is revealed in the quality of sustainable relationships we seek to participate in." Anonymous

"I must teach you in truth & logic, not just spirit, because what you understand in logic can become yours." Rev. Sun Myung Moon

"I have come to explain to blacks, whites & all races that because God's dispensation is going a particular direction, they must harmonize with each other. Americans have difficulties going over the racial barrier. If I were white, they would listen to me." Rev. Sun Myung Moon

"Taken objectively, morality is in itself practical, for it is the totality of the unconditionally binding laws according to which we *ought* to act, & once one has acknowledged the authority of its concept of duty, it would be utterly absurd to continue wanting to say one *cannot* do his duty." Emmanuel Kant

Kant is so rational & reasonable in his assertion. Rationally considered, within the confines of certain values defining the nature of the relationships & their priority to human life, meaning & prosperity, it is not even a 'duty' we are saddled with but rather a joy. In time, a life offered as a measure of gratitude. A celebration of self, fully realized within community, as its most suitable venue for human expression & meaning to be communicated & shared.

Yet, we are born into a world of unimaginable conflict & human created & sustained interpersonal & environmental harm.

If we understood the value & purpose of law, then we would also allow our conscience to assume the role it can only rationally play & serve not only the individual but the collective totality of humanity in its need for civility & the control of deviance that creates harm.

Jesus was aided in his conclusions by being born into a culture that was defined by its stipulation that to be human, required such a state of commitment to others, that our very identity, as an individual, as an individual within community with equal status to all others, we needed to 'act' in ways that secure a particular quality of relationship. Part of a covenant spanning generations almost beyond memory, this quality of being human, by establishing certain values that identify others as also of the same 'tribe' or family, thus creates a family social & political environment, a society of consequence, because all find their own absolute values mirrored in the face of their neighbor, even they meet for the 1st time, in a land far from home.

I am Jewish.

I matter. I will always matter.

Therefore... I am loved.

Hence, God matters to me...

The question that then emerges in this enlightened state?

What measure then 'my' gratitude?

For the infant/child... obedience.

For the child maturing?

Cooperation.

For the child understanding?

New foot prints in attendance, offering the way forward...

This is the example Jesus offered in word, social behavior...& even to his death, his seeking to protect the future the only way his life's choices could offer him, as a child of filial piety would choose.

His death was to affirm that what he had said, was spoken with the authority of one who is in all actuality defending their parent. For what Jesus taught, as the final path to lineage, required a surrendering to not only God's will for humanity, as children, but also the defining moment for self-identification & self-definition. Jesus lived his death the only way he could... as he had lived his life, a life committed helping his siblings on the path steps home.

But as he made absolutely clear, the quality of love, the quality of interpersonal commitment that Jesus knew ONLY established the quality of relationship God sought with humanity, this was absolute.

YET THIS REQUIRED THE FINEST USE OF HUMAN WILL, THE MOST RATIONAL USE OF HUMAN WILL, THE MOST REVEALING OF SUSTAINED DESIRE.

Once we truly, in our heart of hearts, understand & personally embrace the personal & social significance of interpersonal relationships, & the morally significant & corresponding most perfect human means to such wisdom, we discover a quality of commitment, that while not habit initially, will still become the perfect tone, the spring of life, the Philosopher's Stone in whom the 'promise' is not only revealed, but inheritable. By the use of human desire willed to be.

In the confrontation with reality, with the understanding that life is 100% about morally significant, sustainable interpersonal relationships, then the maturing individual, the human who has come to accept their place in the cosmos, these people will look not only at the moment, but they will seek, even in an initial selfishness, the best way forward. Even, if possible, a way to secure the future. The way most profitable.

But a profit meant to be shared, that MUST be shared to even be realized, this profit is the natural profit a true love family produces.

Jesus loved humanity because he understood the quality of investment that God had offered in the Jewish people. But he also realized that the promise, the covenant, was a promise of such a change in the nature of relationships, that the people still needed to play the final scenes needed to create that final hope.

Jesus realized it was a cooperative effort of such quality that was required that the true heart of not only the individual would be revealed, but the true heart of the people.

Yet, the people, individually & as a people who became a nation, did not grasp the significance of life & relationships.

They did not 'get' God's activities, the very nature of the effected integration, that continues to this day.

Moon sought to re-inform humanity… as to God's will, Jesus' efforts & the remaining task & opportunity before us.

For 40 years I did not get Jesus. For 40 years I did not get Moon. Now, I observe two who understood their parent & each other in such form as has never been observed or experienced. With Moon, Jesus had family.

Whom understands my heart, knows my path.

Whom understands my heart, & shares an equal heart, shares our path.

Jesus stated ONLY those who KNEW the true love of enemy, would truly understand God's heart of attendance.

ONLY those who truly KNEW THAT HEART, would never be able to walk away from such a heart.

Hence, ONLY Moon & Jesus offered but one way to heaven, one way home.

The rest of us?

We will follow…UNTIL WE UNDERSTAND.

Then we walk with Jesus & Moon… as equals.

"Peace Starts with Me" as providential & global movement towards community: the need for the certainty of morally significant values informing our emotional identities

(From whom much is given much will be asked...)

"There is still a voice crying out in terms that echo across the generations, saying; Love your enemies, bless them that curse you, pray for them that despitefully use you, that you may be the children of your Father which is in heaven. This love might well be the salvation of our civilization." M.L. King, Jr

"Did not Moses give you the law, and yet none of you keepeth the law? Why go ye about to kill me?" Jesus

"Spiritual power does not come through words, but through practice... In order to enter that realm, you must pray like a crazy person & do things like a crazy person." Rev. Sun Myung Moon

"... the peacemakers will be known as the children of God." Jesus

"Forgiveness is the love I offer my enemy because I have reached the conclusion that life, and therefore love, cannot be fulfilled without my enemy at my table & at my side, but not as my enemy." The Last Spiritual Samurai

Jesus actually brings us full circle in the single quote noted above, offering the insight about the heart such children must then naturally share with their heavenly parent. For it focuses us precisely on the issue facing us as individuals, which in the end, cumulatively, will decide the totality of the social environment we co-create & thus, are forced to share with one another.

Why, of all the qualities described by Jesus, did the issue of a peacemaker offer the 'most desired' status (the children of God as opposed to…) as its natural state? In that same reference to the 'holy of holy's' that would associate us naturally with God, Jesus then further establishes that those who love their enemy, seeking such blessing for them that may aid them on their own spiritual journey, ALSO naturally become recognized as God's own 'children.'

Those of us who imagine a different world, a world in complete moral contrast to the one we occupy & inhabit, we face the same world as those Jesus' words immediately struck. The variance is in the degree of personal, public & political challenge we are forced endure & seek to process. Hence, there is a significant clue & direction that is offered as wisdom, offered by Jesus.

If when enemies are declared, are we quick to take one side or the other? Seeking that one be 'destroyed' & the other 'saved'? When a parent observes their 2 children each seeking to destroy the other, does one, as a parent, REALLY care initially who is or might be at fault or share the greater portion of responsibility?

The challenge is to create a sustainable social state wherein we can rationally, with values that inform any true love family, move the parties towards conflict resolution & eventual restoration.

What is the normal heart of a true parent towards any children suffering in a self-imposed & created hell?

In contrast, what 'psychologically' informing state has the relationship of God & humanity taken? That of such disregard by humanity as to suggest an animus, consciously owned or not?

What has been God's revealed behavior & their informing values? History offers the argument that the exposure to & following a natural response to that offering of God, informs humanity as to the principles & values that allow such a spiritual state of such similarity to God's own nature that God can lay claim to a filial relationship with humanity. Based upon a correlative response in heart & social behavior.

Since God has no physical form, then the ONLY means to embody God is in the shared virtues informing our desire for relationship with others. It is in the nature of those values, integrated into our conscience as the heart of our identity, emotional & rational, that generates a unique expression of those values, just as they have for God.

What values then would inform the child of peace, who was the living embodiment of those values? Jewish history established the only rational 'witness' to the moral significance of God's intervention & integration directly into history, that was effected with Abraham, Moses & finally, in & through Jesus.

The highest socially compelling moral statement of interpersonal moral obligation that was the natural state of 'being Jewish' was the 2 great commandments, that we were to love God with all our concentrated being & only 2nd to that, to love our neighbor as ourselves. This social standard was the core value that created a natural covenant between each Jew born, a core value that defined their very humanity, as children of God or nature. In this scenario, all were recognized as created equal, with a God who, acting as the most intimate of parents, offers all needed, even if not recognized either for its wisdom, or its pragmatic social significance. Hence, to love God, to honor the 10 'words' given Moses, established that every dimension of our lives & living had such moral significance as to affect the very quality of relationship potentially available to humanity as a sustainable state with God.

The ONLY logical, rational & wise addendum that can be naturally added to that standard of interpersonal commitment, from birth to death, is that even in conflict, when others have acted in bad faith, by intent or neglect, to create such harm that any suffers for morally invasive decisions, that we sustain our commitment to ourselves, in service to the commitment to love we have made, as the ultimate 'right' for us, to live by, to define ourselves to the world by.

Hence, the ONLY critical qualification Jesus added to what it meant to be Jewish/human, was the naturally implied value that is required when our children deviate & need further guidance. The value that we label as 'forgiveness', the socially imposed offering NOT to allow the relationship to be further degraded, by adopting whatever response that will de-escalate the situation & sustain our own commitment to further integration as is potentially viable & morally indicated as in the service of restoring the relationship.

This quality of love, the sustained commitment even in the evidence or experience of deviance with its attendant harms, is one that parents utilize a lot with children as they are socialized to accept the inevitability of relationships & their natural & needed moral considerations.

The negative quality of intent & harms has exponentially grown under the authority of adults. Yet Jewish history offers such witness to God & that God's interpersonal behavior & integration that we are fully educated as to the moral potential we are to offer to relationships, as necessity for life & for meaning. Jewish history makes two remarkable demands… to be Jewish & thus, to be human.

1st, to act Jewish. By being Jewish. Hence, to act human; for to be truly human is God's 1st wish & sustained desire. To be human? With Moses, to now come to care such that we commit not to those harms mentioned, but by natural deduction, implies ANY behavior that can contribute to or create harm for others, known or not.

The struggle throughout history, globally, has been the struggle to finds such means to establish a consensus as to the absolute value of the individual human, that the harms so associated with history & current human moral behavior can no longer be justified nor suffered, without social consequence. Such consequence to include the marshalling of such force as to limit the freedom of those whose anti-social behaviors require more radical attendance.

That is NOT to argue a defense of ANY penal system & its administration anywhere in the world.

Today, our voices of rebellion & dissent have offered their lives to the cause of the need for restoring the absolute value to humanity, in part & in its totality. We speak to our feminists, civil rights activists & those others on the front lines of non-violent civil confrontation, to saving our environment, the most logical & yet dismissed universally important value.

Thus, we call for peace.

'We' honor that 1st demand though.

We confront the 1st & most formidable enemy in the mirror.

This is the one we are called 1st to persuade.

To what values will we commit. Beyond the mere comfort zone emotions offer.

Hence, in a supposed Christian nation, then Jesus' words all the more harken to us to honor that original covenant. Love my enemy that I then reveal myself not only as a child of God, but in America, I thus honor the 1st civil right offered every person as their own personal opportunity… to honor my neighbor as "created equal". Created by God & God's nature, hence, as a sibling of one of God's other children, just as being Jewish meant 'acting' as a Jew would thus act. In loving our enemy no less than is rationally is indicated God loved us, as a parent, we emerge both as peacemakers in the heart of our attendance to one another as we encounter conflict but also loving our enemy as we encounter that personally, we offer again the same quality of attendance & commitment that God offered & offers humanity.

Peace starts with me… because I have chosen the ONLY values that the cosmos & the witness of God in history offers as the hope for such individual self-transcendence that the witness created offers the ONLY hope needed to become a center of peace, as a living witness.

The means for restoring peace is as it always was.

The informing values we choose to build our identity, that life is based upon. The same ones that sustain the cosmos, that God exercised… to raise a rebellious & hard-hearted adult generation of children. Rebellious in the habit of anarchy we live as individuals, families & nations.

The 1st home for peace is the true love family.

The family teaches, in word & deed, the value & significance of relationships & their needed optimal values.

The 1st home for peace in a nation is when their families live in peace with one another, even in times of challenge & social insecurity & unrest.

True Family Values, lived in the family but then applied to the social & the political, create the sustainable opportunity for peace not only to emerge, but to become a civil state of such continuity that a new 'culture' is naturally created.

In this social climate & with our individual & collective emotionally significant moral challenges, we need clarity as to the ONLY values that can not only define peace but secure it as an individual, social & political state. These values, rooted in the family tradition that 1st acknowledges the rightful need for unconditional love, BECAUSE WE CHOOSE SO, then becomes the source of our identity & thus, the conscience for guiding all thoughts & emotional states & impulses.

Only in such a socially defined state of being, will we then have the social skills & the needed values & experience, to not only weather the challenges ahead, but to actually prosper in the challenges. In such witness is the hope that Jesus offered in his presence.

History now calls us to no less an important moment. Individually, as ultimate truth bodies of a quality of love commitment not yet a social standard, although promised by America, if yet to be delivered.

In the commitment to love, thus to also repent if one is the deviant, by not only a change of heart, but of sustained behavior, the need for forgiveness is beyond measure.

There is no single greater needed value & social commitment & behavior. God's forgiveness, as Jewish history offers witness, a significant call to arms for humanity, argues that ONLY such sustained love offers always what is needed, for as long needed… as ANY parent knows.

That Martin Luther King, as enlightened as he was, did not truly grasp the significance of God's love to & in history, as one of the greatest social interpreters of Jesus' words, applied to life & living, is disappointing. He did not truly then understand the words of Jesus, left as a challenge/opportunity, & thus, could express such doubt, though it seems he expressed hope.

This is also the failure of white Christian America… yet, they will it so. King sought for ultimate truth… which is the human capacity to care. The evidence of the 'God-seed'.

Actually, as the final key to both being of the quality of peacemaker that God then naturally exposes us as God's children, or by loving when challenged by freedoms that have been so misused as to cause substantial harm to relationships, forgiveness as a commitment to others & to community & relationship is beyond measure. It is the glue between victim & deviant.

It is the glue of God in history. To humanity.

BUT FORGIVENESS IS NOT A RELIGIOUS VALUE, RELIGIOUS PRACTICE NOR RELIGIOUS WAY OF LIFE & LIVING.

It works though, for religious & non-religious alike. For humans. Seeking to be truly human,

It is the final celebration of life, for in its behavior is the key to life, the key to the secret that creates & sustains the human eye.

The nature to always to seek for such sustainable relationship as potential, environment & resources will support.

Jesus taught about peace.

He's still trying to teach about it.

The 1st step is to own who we are & what our values are, & how they are ordered.

Are we still playing 'god' with ourselves or have we placed our heart/desire to care & be cared about, IE, to be in morally significant sustainable relationship, structured so that our commitment to the values of our conscience is the means to defining our value of ourselves, to ourselves & thus to the world?

If our personal world is so morally ordered such that we produce 'peace', not mere niceness, but the genuine offering of such care, that our lives are offered daily to others, as an affirmation of their value, to life itself, then we live not as a beacon of hope, but rather, a beacon of light meant to inspire other beacons to self-potential, until no darkness remains.

If we are not clear about the values that inform the life of peace, in a world of conflict, then we cannot offer but words & emotions. Emotions fade away, words are forgotten.

But principles lived, even in hell, as the last stand for the behavioral defining of the who, what & how we are, with others, as our choice, establishes the value we place on freedom… & offers the only true witness to the possibility of peace, as a human created & shared social experience.

True family values, non-religious, non-political, always family centered, offer the vision, the means & the way. We need will & true heart

Then we will give the ONLY witness to peace that matters. IN HOW & WHY WE RESPOND & INTERFACE WITH ALL OTHERS, EVEN OUR ENEMIES.

Peace starts with me… in the values I choose to give witness to the value I place on myself, as my offering to you, to honor you; offering the all of who I am, all I have, all I can be.

This is the peace I offer you.

The greatest threat to world peace: Trump's 'Christian' America as the failure to defend the true values of America, to morally confront Russia & China

"I am predicting that in the next seven years America will experience incredible decline & degradation, even more than today. Today the churches are irresponsible." Rev. Sun Myung Moon

"The well-being of the family should come before that of the individual; the nation should come before the family, the world before the nation." Rev. Sun Myung Moon

"The purpose of the chosen nation is... to save the world. And God raised up Christianity for the same purpose... to save the world." Rev. Sun Myung Moon
"...just as Jesus willingly gave his life so that the world might live, God wanted all Christians to be willing to give themselves for the salvation of the world. However, today,

Christians of the world are not even close to realizing this heart of God." Rev. Sun Myung Moon

"When the individual & the families which transcend racial & national barriers gather together to create a church, a society & a nation, that nation will become God's ideal nation for all peoples." Rev. Sun Myung Moon

America is a microcosm of the world. Transcending nationality & race. America has created a model for the ideal world... the blessing never comes alone; it comes with responsibility. If one forsakes the responsibility, one forsakes God's blessing... Is it not true that the signs of such decline are already apparent in America today? Beloved American people, the time has come for us to repent. God is crying out to the world." Rev. Sun Myung Moon.

American Christianity as a threat to world peace, existing as a failure to confront the reality of communism as it still seeks to advance its global power base? I am sure there will be a knee-jerk response to such a declaration. But does the affirmative statement deserve our respectful consideration? Is there a morally significant vacuum between the promise of America & her deliverance? Or is this merely another example of the quality of rhetorical give & take that is not only offered, but expected in the current social, civil & political climate? To criticize, to dominate & humiliate? But...

If the statement is even remotely possible, then in the interest of universal justice, including for the people of those countries, our intellectual & heartistic integrity are under judgment if we allow no consideration to crease our brows.

The 1st level or tier of understanding is that we cannot defeat, control or deny these countries militarily nor economically or ideologically. We cannot defeat them ideologically because our main moral operating system is determined by the morality of the economic system we have embraced... not a free-market economy but a capitalistic one. This places profit over people, creating an economic form of slave system, people the last resource to be 'farmed' for its wealth, a wealth generated by sustaining the truly wealthy as they are accustomed to.

I don't accept the idea that it is really a free-market economy because of all the resources that are brought to bear to 'force' a culture of consumerism, rather than a culture of creation & creativity. Advertising, the focused attempt to create a sustainable addiction that relieves people of as much of their earnings as can be reasonably be realized. Hence, the 'science' of willful manipulation of others, for the very express purpose to ONLY realize profit for the wealthiest.

Today, corporations are the new slave owners... a slavery assumed a right because it provides some benefits not associated with slavery in the past.

Like leisure time, rights to property ownership, a 'pay for labor' relationship.

But if you want to understand the underlying principle? Look at the wealth of the Walmart family & stock holders versus the pay scale of its workforce. The noonday sun reveals what we did not truly grasp & now, everything becomes clear

The 1st & ONLY moral premise of capitalism is the inherent 'right' to profit. There is no such premise pre-established in capitalism. It is the very nature of the purpose for defining relationships in such terms that led to the idea as not only a social nicety, but it became its own moral argument.

The premise? ""I" have rights to personal, social & political benefits that need not be shared with the general populace. My effort, time & resources being of a different quality than any others.

How am I free if I cannot take advantage of the relationships around me?"

Paradoxically, that's exactly what the communist ultimately considers in his world view. That others exist to serve his purpose.

When we consider the underlying values in operation between Marxism of any ilk & capitalism as it is embraced, articulated & even legally defended in America, corporations even gaining citizenship of a quality not shared by the poor & colored peoples, we realize that corporations are soulless enterprises not founded on the premise "ALL... ARE CREATED EQUAL" & THUS ASSUME A RIGHT & ENTTITLEMENT TO SUCH EXCEPTIONAL TREATMENT, EVEN ECONOMICALLY, AS THEY DEEM THEIRS & THEIRS ALONE.

The wealthiest billionaires made billions more during the pandemic. THIS IS THEIR PATRIOTISM... THIS IS THEIR APPRECIATION OF THE WORKERS... JUST LIKE IN EVERY COMMUNIST COUNTRY... ONLY THE STANDARD OF LIVING IS A LITTLE BETTER... JUST ENOUGH.

The ultimate slavery is that which is designed to offer the greatest unearned benefit to a self-defined elite & thus, properly entitled, without the masses objecting... even maybe becoming worshipful of our 'masters'. Like the Kardashions... Trumps... who then lord it over us.

That is a godless ideological valuation... applied to the citizens of a nation endowed & entitled NOT to be exploited, EVEN FOR PROFIT. But we have been told that America protects such a value system jealously... the NEW power base that will be taken into account... by paying for the opportunity.

The American dream has been redefined... THE NEW, REFORMED AMERICA, IS NOW ONLY ABOUT THE ACQUISITION & SPENDING OF WEALTH.

No longer a beacon to the down trodden. No longer a witness to what is REALLY possible for a nation & its people, but a vision of eternal competition & adversity.

In such a civil state, then EVERY PERSON IS A PERSON OF OPPORTUNITY, TO BE EXPLOITED FOR WHATEVER AVAILABLE PROFIT THAT MIGHT BE MADE... THIS BEING THE 1ST CIVIL RIGHT DEFINED BY CAPITALISM. SUCH PUBLIC VALUES NOT REQUIRING WE ACKNOWLEDGE NOR HONOR ANY NATIONAL PLEDGE, TO SUCH EFFECT AS TO HONOR ALL OTHERS AS OUR EQUAL. AND THEREFORE, SOMEHOW DESERVING OF ANY OTHER CONSIDERATION THAN THOSE THAT SERVE OUR OWN INTERESTS.

This is the same, natural philosophical premise that communism offers. Neither offers a morality owed god nor man. Both operate under the false premise of 'offering a greater good for the services rendered'. Both then demand that an earned 'entitlement' beyond the measure offered others, is thus due those MOST committed to such values & social principles. The communists of the ruling party on the one side of the nationalist agenda coin & the capitalists & the 6% wealthy on the other side of the coin.

Both exist on the backs of the rest of the populaces. Each maintains such social forces & support as to keep dissension & rebellion under such control as not to threaten the current economic social, & therefore political order.

THE ONLY TRUE MEANS TO CONFRONT COMMUNISM, CHINESE OR RUSSIAN, IS TO CREATE A SOCIETY WHERE THE WEALTH THAT IS GENERATED IS SHARED AS A MORALLY DEFINING ASPECT OF WHAT IT MEANS TO BE AN AMERICAN, & A HUMAN. That wealth includes such natural civil wealth as promised by the nation, as well as the wealth produced in the daily efforts of its peoples.

Hence, profit is not the domain of the few, but the fruits of the labors that the laborers share. In this, then each person comes to value their own offering, because it is producing a benefit for others.

Only in a civil society where all are equally vested in creating support for the greater community, as a natural statement of life & living in that community, can people not only be free to explore all it means to be human, but it also defines the social climate of creation & coordination of people towards the needs of people. In toto.

It should be a national shame the way people are forced to live… the fact we have hungry & those who cannot obtain the natural medical care EVERY person deems is their natural right, as a human, as part of a human community.

ASK ANY INDIVIDUAL WHETHER MEDICAL CARE IS NOT A HUMAN NECESSITY & THAT, AS A HUMAN, WE SHOULD NATURALLY SEEK TO PROVIDE SUCH SERVICES FOR OURSELVES.

Any parent who could not afford medical care for their children who are in serious need, while all around them are the most amazing hospitals, equipment & trained & motivated personnel, would naturally wonder what kind of society allows children to suffer when they need not…

It is a concern that should haunt EVERY parent & ANY CHRISTIAN who dares use the term.

No less so hunger…

Hundreds of millions of dollars are used to get a person elected to office who then proceeds to forget everyone except his/her own special interests or pet projects & agendas.

That the majority of Americans support national medical for all & Republicans refuse to consider it, calling it socialism & the next step to communism, is not listening to its people, but rather assuming to decide for us, what is best for us. This arrogance is unconscionable.

Yet these same 'Americans', being part of the rich elite, then continue to reduce the tax burden of the wealthy & corporations, that continue to take the people for everything they can sustainably manage.

"I" didn't approve corporations making billions in profit, but paying no income tax & getting a refund…

DID YOU? DID YOU AUTHORIZE SUCH GREED TO BE REWARDED… THAT NOW INCREASES THE NATIONAL DEBT 'YOU' ARE RESPONSIBLE FOR… & YOUR CHILDREN… & AS WILL BE BURDENED YOUR GRAND & GREAT GRANDCHILDREN. While THEIR grandchildren will still regale us with their wealth, how they abuse it & why we should be so entertained by it. Like we do now…

Americans, when they ACT as Americans are directed to act, then create a social system that does not encourage, allow nor reward economics based upon exploitation of others, either as laborers nor as consumers. In such a social system, there is no imagining oneself as MORE entitled than others.

THAT PATHWAY COULD ONLY & DID ONLY PRODUCE A MARXISM/COMMUNISM IN REACTION TO & A CAPITALISM THAT ONLY VARIES IN THE DEGREE OF IMAGINED FREEDOM ALLOWED... & FOR THE QUALITY OF PROFIT IT GARNERED FOR THOSE MOST SUCCESSFUL AN IT, BY HOOK OR CROOK.

Yet, communism crossed that bridge, too, of how to extract wealth from a nation not truly wealthy, except by the force it brings to bear on its people 24/7. Such overwhelming force & threat of force that only madmen imagined a competing freedom.

Where communism uses outright force... capitalism uses consumerism as a means to create a sustainable slave force, that also serves as a slave market for most of the products made by the people. There is a sense of a comparative degree of freedom as compared to the rest of the world such that the slavery of one's own position is not as poignantly experienced & thus, noted. Then, it noted & engaged for its potential meaning, requiring interpretation & further action, if any.

With Trump & the Republican Party in control, dominated by millionaires & supported by an uncivil white & white Christian populace, Americans experienced a further degrading of not only their civil rights, but their economic viability continue to be degraded.

A national hourly wage of $7.50 is not just an insult when corporate heads of such work forces make millions each year in wages, benefits & perks; it is an example of modern-day slavery. Think $2000 an hour versus that $7.50. That 250 times more... DON'T THINK YOU'RE SOMONE ELSES 'NIGGER'?

THAT IS THE WAGE RATIO OF BLACK TO WHITE IN THE SOUTH... DURING SLAVERY. THINK ABOUT IT.

Who does most of the low pay positions? Disproportionately women, especially women of color, minorities in general & young people, expecting to pay their own way.

Every Republican president has aided the wealthy & corporations by continually reducing their tax burdens...5 CORPORATIONS MADE 1.14 BILLION IN TAX REFUNDS, THANKS TO TRUMP'S TAX RELIEF. HOW DO COMPANIES THAT MAKE BILLIONS IN PROFIT, PAY NO TAXES & YET, GET BILLIONS IN REFUNDS?

This is the America now being hijacked by corporations & the wealthy. This is what we offer the world, as an alternative to communism... all a matter of degree.

Yet, used properly, for the benefit of all her people, & then also to the world, America CAN OFFER THE ONLY MORAL, ECONOMIC IDEOLOGICAL ARGUMENT THAT COMMUNISM & NO OTHER FORM OF DICATORSHIP CAN ARGUE WITH NOR OFFER COMPETITION TO... FOR THE CREATIVITY & PSYCHOLOGICAL HEALTH OF ITS PEOPLE IT WILL NATURALLY ENGENDER.

BUT AN ECONOMIC SYSTEM WHERE ALL SHARE IN THE REWARDS, NOT JUST THE TOP OR MIDDLE. WHERE BEING A 'CITIZEN', WITH OTHER LIKE CITIZENS, IS EVERYTHING, TO EVERYONE.

This is the world Jesus asks us to create, inhabit & share with others... because we can.

Without such values defining the character & heart of a people? There is no confrontation possible with communism or any other evil form of leading a people.

America IS THE ONLY HOPE THE WORLD HAS... FOR THE VALUES DEMANDED 1ST BY THE 1ST CIVIL RIGHT & SOCIALLY DEFINED AMERICAN VALUE... THAT ALL ARE CREATED EQUAL, & THUS, AS A

NATIONAL FAMILY, WILL SHARE IN THAT EXPERIENCE IN ALL WAYS MEANINGFUL... PERSONAL, PUBLIC & POLITICAL Including economically.

When racists & sexists & those not treasuring the environment as stewards, rather acting as profit exploiters, are not the norm in America? When Americans ACT AS AMERICANS...

Communism will have no justification left...

It won't be just a wall being torn down.

Which we socialists were the most responsible for it coming down... but Americans don't know that story. Yet.

Conclusion's

"All we say to America is, "Be true to what you say on paper..." Martin L. King, Jr

"The developed nations of the world should feel that they have been blessed by God for the purpose of helping others. They must be willing to offer themselves for the underdeveloped nations of the world. If the prosperous nations do not think in loftier terms than the desire for profits, their prosperity will slip away in spite of their efforts to retain it." Rev. Sun Myung Moon

"obligation: a binding contract, promise, responsibility, etc." Webster's New World Dictionary & Thesaurus

"If freedom is to be extended, it must discipline itself both personally & communally. On the personal level this means developing a unity of purpose so that choosing & action are harmonious for the self. This also involves a communal awareness & concern for the individual is part of society. Thus, unity has normative features in conjunction with freedom." John K Roth

"To treat someone civilly means to remain a respectful distance from encroaching on his rights, & to accord him the dignity appropriate to a bearer of equal rights. Civility is one glue of a community of a specific kind, a community of bearers of equal individual rights." Clifford Orwin

"...(citizenship) implies membership in a community defined by a common substantive end, more comprehensive, more dignified, more authoritative than the particular ends of private individuals." Clifford Orwin

"...even as citizenship requires civility, so civility points beyond itself to certain permanent & objective moral standards-to the nature of "civil government," &, higher still, to the moral & theoretical concerns of what is rightly called civilization." Charles R Kesler

"Civility is an attitude & a mode of action which attempts to strike a balance between conflicting demands & conflicting interests. Liberal democracy is especially in need of the virtue of civility because liberal democracy is more prone to bring latent conflicts into actuality." Edward Shils

"...when there is intense verbal abuse against groups because of race, religion, nationality or language, it becomes difficult, if not impossible, to maintain the principle & the practice of freedom of speech." Robert A. Goldwin

(We MUST consent to inquire at least once... 'IS THERE a Mc Donald's fast food form of moral & ethical path to peace'... then we open our eyes.)

"The state of peace must therefore be *established,* for the suspension of hostilities does not provide the security of peace, & unless this security is pledged by one neighbor to another (which can happen only in a state of *lawfulness),* the latter, from whom security has been requested, can treat the former as enemy." Emmanuel Kant

"...it is time to forsake our age & its adolescent furies..."
Albert Camus

The 'Alpha' social agent recognizes the primacy of morally significant sustainable relationships to life, living & the quality & prosperity possible, but as a shared potential, requiring the individual own a state of sustained moral commitment to civil integration, realized in relationship & community.

The time is ripe for national & global bodies to be concerned about the psychological potential & health of its citizens & their moral

needs to aid in the social education &
civilization of the next generation.

To those 'spirits' already on that journey,
seeking wisdom as they seek community, it is
to them that this book is properly &
honorably dedicated.
It is they, together, who will create a NEW
future...

"What is holy? These are holy; you go to bed
when you want to sleep, you eat when you
want to eat, & you play when you want to
play." Rev Sun Myung Moon

"With this joy, through long struggle, we shall remake the
soul of our time..." Albert Camus